GAZ

A CITY OF MAN

(FROM THE FAMILY OF NOAH TO … DAY)

BY

THEODORE EDWARD DOWLING, D.D.

ARCHDEACON IN SYRIA;
CANON OF ST. GEORGE'S COLLEGIATE CHURCH, JERUSALEM;
COMMISSARY FOR EASTERN CHURCH INTERCOURSE WITHIN THE ANGLICAN BISHOPRIC IN JERUSALEM

PUBLISHED UNDER THE DIRECTION OF THE TRACT COMMITTEE

LONDON
SOCIETY FOR PROMOTING CHRISTIAN KNOWLEDGE
NORTHUMBERLAND AVENUE, W.C.; 43, QUEEN VICTORIA STREET, E.C.
BRIGHTON: 129, NORTH STREET
NEW YORK: E. S. GORHAM
1913

TO

DONALD A. COLES, M.D.

I DEDICATE THIS BOOKLET

WHICH WOULD NEVER HAVE BEEN WRITTEN

WITHOUT HIS ASSISTANCE AND

SYMPATHY

PREFACE

On Tuesday in Easter week, 1912, accompanied by the Rev. J. Khadder, Assistant Chaplain of St. Luke's Mission, Haifa, I left that town for El-Kaisâriyeh (Cæsarea), where we were entertained at the Orthodox Greek rented house belonging to a Bosnian landlord. On reaching Jaffa I secured a fresh carriage on April 12, for Gaza, reaching that city in nine and a half hours,—an unusually quick journey. During my visit of ten days there I was the guest of the Rev. Dr. and Mrs. Sterling, in the Church Missionary Society's compound. Nothing could have exceeded their kind hospitality, and I am greatly indebted to them for valuable local information. Mrs. Sterling used her typewriter for producing my Chapter XXI on the "History of the C.M.S. Gaza Mission," 1878–1913.

The aged and scholarly German, Father Gatt, one of the Latin Clergy attached to the Roman Catholic Patriarchate of Jerusalem, who came to Gaza thirty-three years ago from Austria, and ministers to eighty souls, lent me three printed articles on Gaza, and cheerfully added to my limited knowledge of the city. He mentioned that a History of Gaza has been printed by Dr. Martin A. Meyer, and published at New York in 1907, but I had not the advantage of seeing this book. After my manuscript was completed early in 1912, I procured a copy, and have during 1913 taken the liberty of incorporating some additional information from its contents, for which I am grateful.

Mr. A. A. Knesevich, H.B.M. Consular Agent at Gaza—of Austrian parentage—lent me five of his official printed Reports, notes from which are included under the heading of "The Key of Syria," Chapter XIX.

It will be noticed in Chapter XVII that I am also indebted to Mr. Emil G. Knesevich, for photographs of an "Old Sarcophagus at Gaza," but unfortunately, they have not proved sufficiently clear for reproduction.

Mr. Habeebel Khouri, the C.M.S. Catechist, not only accompanied me to the Great Mosque, but supplied me with information.

Miss Kate Sandreczka translated articles in German bearing on the history of the city.

At a short distance from Mayoumas, the maritime quarter of Gaza, on the north-west side, are the ruins of Thedah (or Tedûn) the site of the ancient Hellenistic town of Anthedon, lately discovered by Père Gatt. Alexander Jannæus took it along with Gaza. In company with Dr. Sterling I visited this spot, enveloped in sand, on April 18, where we found broken pieces of marble, ornamented glazed pottery, and ancient glass scattered in every direction. Excavations for hewn stone have not been infrequent here.

Augustus gave this port to Herod the Great, who rebuilt it, and changed its name into that of Agrippeion, after his friend Marcus Agrippa.

Anthedon was an early archiepiscopal see, in Palestina Prima, and I am familiar with the few specimens of its coinage during the reigns of Elagabalus (A.D. 218–222), and Alexander Severus (A.D. 222–235). Since the days of the Muslim occupation there is no mention of this town, and its name does not appear in Holy Writ.

Among the Hellenistic towns in Schürer's *The Jewish People in the Time of Jesus Christ*, Division II, vol. i, pp. 72-3, there is additional information on Anthedon, (Ἀνθηδών).[1]

On the following afternoon I visited Djebel el-Mountâr, a hill, two hundred and seventy feet high, about two miles from the city towards the south-east. It is the "hill that is before Hebron" (Judges xvi. 3) to which Samson carried during the night one of the gates of the city. He did not carry the gate as far as Hebron, which is upwards of twelve hours' ride, but he went in the direction of Hebron. It was a superhuman feat to tear away the gate posts, and carry them across to the top of a neighbouring hill.

It is interesting to compare Josephus' account of this episode with that of the sacred historian. In his *Antiquities*, Book V, section 10, Whiston's edition, the following passage occurs—

"Samson held the Philistines in contempt, and came to Gaza, and took up his lodgings in a certain inn. When the rulers of Gaza were informed of his coming hither, they seized upon the gates, and placed men in ambush about them, that he might not escape without being perceived; but Samson, who was acquainted with their contrivances against him, arose about midnight, and ran by force upon the gates, with their posts and beams, and the rest of their wooden furniture, and carried them away on his shoulders, and bore them to the mountain that is over Hebron, and there laid them down."[2]

[1] See also *The Historical Geography of the Holy Land*, 1902, p. 189.

[2] See Chapter XV on the architectural character of the Gaza Temple of Dagon.

The hill is covered with Muslim tombs, and overtopped by a Weli, dedicated to Aly-el-Mountâr—"Aly the Tower of Defence." Marnas was originally worshipped here.

The extensive view well repays the ascent, for on a clear day the mountains of Hebron may be seen. The sea is visible. There is a fine view of Gaza, and the extensive plain is under cultivation. Due south on the coast is the site Deir el-Belah (Convent of Dates), where the body of St. Hilarion was said to be finally buried.

Napoleon Bonaparte camped here with his army one night towards the end of February 1799, and on the following morning continued his march towards Jaffa.

I gladly avail myself of this opportunity to express my delight and astonishment at finding such an exceptionally well managed native girls' school in the C.M.S. compound. And no wonder, when Miss Smithies instructs the four native female teachers, the two monitresses, and the four half-monitresses, twice every weekday! My experience is that the most useful boys' school in Syria is at Sidon, under the American Congregationalists, and Gaza may well be proud of its girls' school, for there is nothing to approach its varied excellence in Palestine.

The misgovernment of Gaza and its district is worse under the Young Turks than under the late *régime*. But the C.M.S. mission work in the Gaza compound is indeed a bright spot in the city, and the persistent Christian teaching—boldly proclaimed—is bearing fruit in unexpected quarters. Holy enthusiasm is bound to tell in the course of time.

It seems more common for the younger boys of the poorer class in Gaza, than in other parts of Palestine, to have their hair fancifully shaved. One has a tuft on the top of the skull; another a small ring of hair. Some small fellahin boys have the hair growing quite long over the back of the neck, while the whole crown is well shaved. The tuft of hair implies that Mohammed will pull them into heaven. Another theory is that this tuft is left for the benefit of the resurrection angel, who will facilitate their resurrection from the grave.

It will be noticed that I have made free use of Dr. George Adam Smith's *Historical Geography of the Holy Land*, twelfth edition, 1906.

Mr. Miltiades N. Assimacopoulos, B.C., of Acre (Ptolemais), has rendered me invaluable assistance in looking up references, arranging the Index, and type-writing portions of the manuscript for the press.

The indulgent reader will kindly remember that this book has been compiled under peculiar circumstances. There is no public reference library in this Muslim town of Haifa, and the authorities who have been consulted on Gaza are not agreed as to several dates in its chequered history.

My thanks are due to the Rev. R. J. E. Boggis, B.D., St. Mary Magdalene's Vicarage, Barnstaple, for carefully correcting the proof-sheets, as well as those of *The Orthodox Greek Patriarchate of Jerusalem.*

St. Luke's Mission, Haifa-under-Mt. Carmel, Palestine, September 5, 1913.

CONTENTS

APPENDICES

ILLUSTRATIONS

[1] Reduced and reproduced by permission of The Palestine Exploration Fund.

AUTHORITIES CONSULTED

A Dictionary of Classical Antiquities, etc., 1891.
ALFORD'S *Greek Testament*, vol. ii, 1861.
Apocrypha, revised version of, 1895.
BÆDEKER'S *Palestine and Syria*, 1906.
BARING-GOULD, REV. S., *Lives of the Saints.*
BELL'S *The Saints of Christian Art* ("The Great Hermits"), 1902.
Bible Educator, The, vols. i and iii (no date).
Bible, Holy, The.
BRIGHT'S *The Age of the Fathers*, 2 vols., 1903.
Cambridge Companion to the Bible, 1905.
CONDER'S *Syrian Stone Lore*, 1886.
CONDER'S *Tent Work in Palestine*, vol. ii, 1878.
Dictionary of Christian Antiquities, vol. i, 1875.
Encyclopædia Britannica, vol. x (ninth edition), 1879.
EUSEBIUS' *Ecclesiastical History*, 1851.
FLINDERS PETRIE'S *Egypt and Israel*, 1911.
GEIKIE'S *The Holy Land and the Bible*, vol. i, 1887.
GUY LE STRANGE'S *Palestine under the Muslims*, 1890.
Handbooks of the C.M.S. Missions. *The Palestine Mission*, 1910.
HASTINGS' *Dictionary of the Bible*, 1904.
HEAD'S *Historia Numorum*, 1887.
HILL'S *Life of Porphyry*, 1913.
Josephus (Whiston's), edited by Dr. Margoliouth, 1906.
Jottings and Snapshots from Gaza, S. Palestine, Nos. 1–3, 1908–1910.
MADDEN'S *Coins of the Jews*, 1881.
MEISTERMANN'S *Fr. Barnabas' New Guide to the Holy Land*, 1907.
METAXAKIS on the Madaba Map, in *Nea Sion*, 1907.

AUTHORITIES CONSULTED

MEYER'S *History of the City of Gaza*, 1907.

MURRAY'S *Dictionary of Christian Biography*, 1911.

MURRAY'S *Handbook of Syria and Palestine*, Part I, 1868.

NEALE'S *History of the Holy Eastern Church*, Part I, 1850.

NEALE'S *History of the Holy Eastern Church*, "The Patriarchate of Alexandria," vol. i, 1847.

NEALE'S *Lent Legends*, 1905.

NEALE'S *The Patriarchate of Antioch*, 1883.

OLIPHANT'S (LAURENCE) *Haifa, or Life in Modern Palestine*, 1887.

PORTER'S *The History of Beirût*, 1912.

PUSEY'S *Commentary on the Minor Prophets*, 1879.

Quarterly Statement of the Palestine Exploration Fund—various.

ROBERTSON'S *History of the Christian Church*, vol. i, 1854.

ROBINSON'S *Biblical Researches in Palestine*, vol. ii, 1856.

SAYCE'S *Patriarchal Palestine*, 1912.

SCHÜRER'S *History of the Jewish People in the time of Christ*, vols. i, ii, 1898.

SMITH'S (GEORGE ADAM) *The Historical Geography of the Holy Land*, 1902.

STEVENSON'S *The Crusaders in the East*, 1907.

WORDSWORTH'S *Greek Testament*, "The Acts of the Apostles," 1860.

WORDSWORTH'S *The Ministry of Grace*, 1901.

GAZA

CHAPTER I

(I) OLD TESTAMENT, (II) DEUTERO-CANONICAL BOOKS, (III) NEW TESTAMENT REFERENCES TO GAZA

THERE are twenty *Old Testament* allusions to Gaza; certainly one reference in the *Deutero-Canonical* books; and one more in the *Acts of the Apostles*.

1. Genesis x. 19.—*The border of the Canaanites was from Sidon, as thou comest to Gerar, unto Gaza.* Thus Gaza is among the earliest of the Canaanitish cities mentioned in Genesis. The reference in this early chapter, which transports us into the dim dawn of human history, is a presumption of its extreme antiquity, and like its distant neighbour Sidon suggests its being among the most ancient cities of the world. Even before Abraham left his fatherland Gaza stood on the southernmost border of Canaan. Its important strategic position on the frontier of Egypt has contributed to its long-continued existence.

Gaza, like Damascus, is mentioned both in the *Book of Genesis*, and in the *Acts of the Apostles*.

2. Joshua x. 41.—*Joshua smote them from Kadesh-barnea even unto Gaza.*

Gaza became celebrated as one of the five royal cities of the Philistines.

Politically, there were five *principal* centres: the

cities of Ashdod; Gaza; Askelon, Gath, and Ekron (1 Sam. vi. 16, 17).

Unlike its neighbours Gath and Askelon, Gaza has survived the various changes of history. Ashdod is now the mud village of Esdûd. The modern name of Askelon is 'Askalân.[1] The site of Gath is uncertain. Ekron is identified with 'Akîr, near a station on the railway from Jaffa to Jerusalem.

3. Joshua xi. 22.—*There were none of the Anakims left in the land of the children of Israel; only in Gaza, in Gath, and in Ashdod, there remained.*

Joshua only partially subdued this remarkable people, who seem to have been akin to the Rephaim and other gigantic races alluded to in the Old Testament. It was not contemplated that, under any circumstances, the "dispossession" alluded to in Numb. xxxiii. 51–3, would be *at once* completed, as plainly intimated in Exodus xxiii. 29, 30.[2]

4. Joshua xv. 20 and 47.—*This is the inheritance of the tribe of Judah . . . Gaza with her towns and her villages.*

Although the tribe of Judah, to whom the city fell, subdued it, yet they appear to have held it but a short time.[3]

5. Judges i. 18.—*Judah took Gaza with the coast thereof.*

This victory of Judah *alone* over the chief cities of Palestine is a proof that the subsequent oppression of

[1] In Judith ii. 28; 1 Macc. x. 86, xi. 60; both in A.V. and R.V. Askelon is called Ascalon.

[2] Ethnology of the Bible. *The Bible Educator*, vol. iii, pp. 197–200.

[3] See also *The Historical Geography of the Holy Land*, 1902, p. 189.

Israel by the Philistines was due to the sins of Israel. The five lords of the Philistines not only regained possession of their own territory, but also increased in strength, and, at length, extended their jurisdiction in turn over the Israelites (Judges iii. 1-5).

"The Philistines appear to have come into the maritime plain of Syria either shortly before or shortly after Israel left Egypt."—*G. A. Smith.*

6. Judges vi. 3-5.—*When Israel had sown, the Midianites came up, and the Amalekites, and the children of the east, . . . and they encamped against them . . . till thou come unto Gaza, and left no sustenance for Israel.*

A new apostasy, punished by the oppression of Midian, is here introduced. This invasion came from the south-east and extended over the whole land "unto Gaza" in the south-west.

7. Judges xvi. 1-4.—*Then went Samson to Gaza.*

8. Judges xvi. 21-31.—*The Philistines took him, and put out his eyes, and brought him down to Gaza.*

Gaza had been the scene of Samson's sin (verses 1 and 2). It is now made the scene of his punishment.

After forty years of oppression, Samson appeared as the champion and avenger of his people. The tragic close of his life has given Gaza an imperishable fame.

> "Samson hath quit himself
> Like Samson, and heroically has finished
> A life heroic."—*Milton.*

The famous Dagon, or the "Fish-god," who had a temple at Gaza (Judges xvi. 21-5), was a national, and not merely a local god among the Philistines. During the Maccabean wars Jonathan destroyed the temple of

Dagon at Azotus (1 Macc. x. 84). He was eminently the god of agriculture.

9. 1 Samuel vi. 17.—*The golden emerods which the Philistines returned for a trespass offering unto the* LORD *. . . for Gaza one.*

During the "seven months" the sacred chest was, no doubt, located in each of the five Philistine cities, in the Dagon temple, which each of the cities possessed.

The god Dagon was worshipped at Gaza and Ashdod, and the goddess Derketo at Askelon. It has been assumed that the two divinities were akin. According to Lucian, Derketo was worshipped under the form of a woman with the body and tail of a fish, fish being sacred to her, and was probably identical with Atargatis, in 2 Macc. xii. 26. Hence Dagon was supposed to have been the male counterpart of Derketo. This view, however, Prof. Sayce now repudiates, preferring to regard Dagon as a purely agricultural deity.

10. 2 Kings xviii. 8.—*Hezekiah smote the Philistines, even unto Gaza, and the borders thereof.*

The entire land of Philistia was ravaged by the Judæan forces.

After continual wars under the Judges, with Saul (1 Sam. xiv. 52, xxxi. 1), and David (2 Sam. v. 17–25), the Philistines appear to have been subdued by the latter, and Gaza became the border of Solomon's kingdom "on this side of the river" (1 Kings iv. 21, 24). In verse 24 Azzah, or rather 'Azza, is the more correct spelling of Gaza. There is a reference to Gaza under the name of Azzah in Deut. ii. 23, and 1 Chron. vii. 28 (R.V.). With this exception the R.V. adopts the reading Gaza.

In Joshua xv. 47 "the river of Egypt" (A.V.) refers to the desert stream, one mile wide, which still occasionally flows in the valley called El Arish, twelve hours' ride south of Gaza. Palm trees are abundant in the bed of this torrent. See Gen. xv. 18; Joshua xv. 4; 1 Kings viii. 65; Is. xxvii. 12.

11. 1 Chronicles vii. 28.—*And their possessions were . . . unto Gaza and the towns thereof.*

The passage refers to Ephraim's habitations, but this is a doubtful reading. The Revised Version of the Old Testament reads *Azza*, in the margin *Ayyah.*

12. Jeremiah xxv. 17–20.—*Then took I the cup at the* LORD'S *hand, and made all the nations to drink, unto whom the* LORD *had sent me: to wit . . . all the kings of the land of the Philistines, and Ashkelon, and Azzah, and Ekron, and the remnant of Ashdod.*

The words describe the act of the prophet as in the ecstacy of vision. One by one the nations are made to drink of the cup of the wrath of Jehovah. Among them are four of the cities of the Philistines, including Gaza.

13. Jeremiah xlvii. 1.—*The word of the* LORD *that came to Jeremiah the prophet against the Philistines, before that Pharaoh smote Gaza.*

This passage probably refers to Pharaoh Necho II's (610–594 B.C.) first advance to Carchemish in 609 B.C. Having defeated and killed Josiah, King of Judah, at Megiddo, he advanced to the Euphrates, and on his return smote the city of Kadytis which is probably Gaza.

14. Jeremiah xlvii. 5.—*Baldness is come upon Gaza.*

The reference is to the destruction which Nebuchadrezzar inflicted upon the whole Syrian seaboard from Sidon to Gaza after Pharaoh Necho's defeat at Carchemish in 604 B.C. (Jeremiah xlvi. 2).

Gaza had to recognise the supremacy of Babylon. "Baldness" is the sign of mourning (Micah i. 16).

Destroyed again and again, its situation has always secured its being rebuilt.

15. Amos i. 6, 7.—*Thus saith the* Lord; *for three transgressions of Gaza, and for four, I will not turn away the punishment thereof; because they carried away the whole captivity, to deliver them up to Edom: but I will send a fire on the wall of Gaza, which shall devour the palaces thereof.*

The proceedings of Philistia against Judah are here represented by Gaza as the principal city. See 2 Chron. xxi. 16–17, which implies a veritable sack of Jerusalem. The extreme barbarity of which Judah complained was that her children were delivered up to her old implacable enemy, Edom.

16. Zephaniah ii. 4.—*Gaza shall be forsaken . . . and Ekron shall be rooted up.*

There is a play on the meaning of these words, "Gaza (Azzah = strong) shall be forsaken (âzab)" and "Ekron (deep-rooting) shall be rooted up (âkar)," similar to that in Micah i. 10, *et seq.*

The chastisement of Philistia is prophesied in verses 4–7. "The fulfilment of the prophecy is not tied down to time" (Pusey, *Minor Prophets*).

17. Zechariah ix. 5.—*Gaza shall see it, and be very sorrowful. . . . The king shall perish from Gaza.*

Well might Gaza fear and tremble on hearing of the destruction of Tyre.

Gaza was taken by Alexander the Great after a siege of two months.[1] When he subdued it, he ordered all the men to be slaughtered without quarter, and carried away all the women and children into bondage, 332 B.C. New

[1] See Josephus, *Antiq. Jews*, XI. 8, 4, section 325.

colonists settled within the city, which now ceased to be a Philistine centre, only to become a Greek one.

Gaza must have been at this time a city of great strength, for Alexander's Greek engineers acknowledged their inability to invent engines of sufficient power to batter its massive walls. Alexander himself was severely wounded in the shoulder during a sortie of this garrison.

Special mention is made by Hegasias (a contemporary of Alexander) of the "King" of Gaza being brought alive to Alexander after the captivity of the city. The name of the governor of the garrison at Gaza was Babemeses.

In Pusey's *Commentary on the Minor Prophets*—Amos i. 6, 7; Zephaniah ii. 4; Zechariah ix. 5, there is much additional information concerning the prophecies against Gaza.

Gaza is there described as first Canaanite; then Philistine; then, at least after Alexander, Edomite; after Alexander Jannæus, Greek; conquered by Abu-Bekr the first Khalif, it became Mohammedan; it was desolated in their civil wars until the crusaders rebuilt its fort; then again Mohammedan.

1. 1 Maccabees xi. 61, 62.—*From whence he* [Jonathan] *went to Gaza, but they of Gaza shut him out; wherefore he laid siege unto it, and burned the suburbs thereof with fire, and spoiled them. Afterward, when they of Gaza made supplication unto Jonathan, he made peace with them, and took the sons of their chief men for hostages.*

After the death of Alexander, the territory of Gaza became for two centuries the battlefield between the Egyptian, Syrian, and Jewish armies. Twice (315 and 306 B.C.) Antigonus took the city from Ptolemy I.

The latter re-took it twice at the point of the sword, and for a century it remained under the power of Egypt.

The Syrians again devastated it in 198 B.C.

Jonathan Maccabeus (the wary), the Jewish leader and high priest (161–143 B.C.) laid siege to its suburbs, and forced the inhabitants to sue for terms (1 Macc. xi. 61, 62).

2. 1 Maccabees xiii. 43–8.—*In those days Simon camped against Gaza,*[1] *and besieged it round about; he made also an engine of war, and set it by the city,*[2] *and battered a certain tower, and took it.*

Simon the Maccabee, Ethnarch, and High Priest, 142–135 B.C., laid siege to the fortress of Gaza, and expelled the heathen inhabitants. Shortly afterwards he appointed his third son, John Hyrcanus I, as commander-in-chief of all his forces.

1. Acts viii. 26.—*And the angel of the* LORD *spake unto Philip, saying, Arise, and go toward the south unto the way that goeth down from Jerusalem unto Gaza, which is desert.*

There is only one New Testament reference to Gaza, and it has given rise to much controversy.

The pronoun αὕτη may either relate to ὁδὸν (way) or to Gaza. If the former, then it is the *way* which is

[1] The Revised Version of the Apocrypha reads "against Gazara." See Josephus, *The Jewish War*, Book I, Chap. II, section 2 (50).

[2] In the Old Testament the distinction between a town and a village is not generally defined. The former, as a rule, was an inhabited place surrounded by a wall. The latter, one that is not so enclosed (Lev. xxv. 29-31). Towns themselves, however, are also sometimes distinguished as walled and unwalled (Deut. iii. 5; Esther ix. 19). The New Testament and Josephus uniformly distinguish between πόλις and κώμη (an unwalled village, opposite to a fortified city).—Schürer, II. i. 154.

desert; if the latter, it is the *city*. If we apply it to the city it is difficult to reconcile the statement with the facts of history; unless we regard the phrase "which is desert" as a parenthetic explanation of St. Luke's written soon after the destruction of Gaza by the Jews in A.D. 66.

Some refer ἔρημος to the *ancient city* destroyed by Alexander, and affirm that the new city occupied a different site.

The words αὕτη ἐστὶν ἔρημος, however, were probably intended to describe the Roman highway on which St. Philip the Evangelist should find the Eunuch. There were then, as now, several roads leading from Jerusalem to Gaza. Two traversed the rich plain of Philistia; but one ran to Eleutheropolis (Beit Jibrîn), and thence direct through an uninhabited waste to Gaza.

See Alford's *Greek Testament* on Acts viii. 26, and Wordsworth's *Greek Testament* on the same passage, which he thus explains: "Go by the road which leads to Gaza—which is desert; Almighty GOD has something for thee to do there. He can enable thee to do the work of an Evangelist, not only in the city of Samaria, but in the wilderness of Philistia."

Note on Acts viii. 38.—Deacons in the early Church, notwithstanding the precedent of St. Philip, were not usually allowed to baptise alone. Wordsworth's *The Ministry of Grace*, p. 161.

CHAPTER II

SUMMARY OF CHIEF EVENTS RELATING TO GAZA [1] FROM 1503 B.C. to A.D. 1913

Section I (1503 B.C. to 30 B.C.) [2]

1503–1449 B.C.—Eighteenth Dynasty. In the twenty-second year of his reign, 1481 B.C. (according to Sayce), Thothmes III made his first determined attempt to subdue Canaan. Gaza was occupied with much difficulty. The fortress of the Prince of Gaza is mentioned in the great expedition of Thothmes III.

c. 1444 B.C.—Eighteenth Dynasty. Amen-hetep II, successor of Thothmes III, has hieroglyphic inscriptions in Gaza, which have been lately discovered. They show that a temple had been built by this Egyptian king to the goddess An Mut.

c. 1366 B.C.—Nineteenth Dynasty. Seti Mer-en Ptah I, the father of Rameses II, drove the Beduins before him from the frontiers of Egypt to those of Canaan, and established a line of fortresses and walls along "the way of the Philistines," which ran by the way of the shore to Gaza (Sayce).

1348–1281 B.C.—Nineteenth Dynasty. Rameses II, User-Maāt-Ra (the Great), continued to hold Gaza till at least 1292, or later.

c. 1225 B.C.—Twentieth Dynasty. Rameses III, Hik-An, captured Gaza, but it does not seem to have remained long in the possession of the Egyptians (Sayce.)

[1] Some of these events in the first section are not referred to either in the Old Testament or the Books of the Maccabees.

[2] Perhaps the earliest notice of Gaza is contained in the Tel-el-Amarna tablets in a letter from a local Governor, who then held it for Egypt.

734–732 B.C.—Tiglath-pileser III, the founder of the second Assyrian Empire, plundered Gaza, and made it subject to Assyria. It soon revolted against its new masters, relying, no doubt, upon help from Egypt, but in vain.

c. 720 B.C.—Hanno, King of Gaza, called to his aid So (Shabaka), King of Egypt (2 Kings xvii. 4), against the Assyrian general Sargon, and commenced that gigantic struggle between Asia and Egypt, of which Gaza was the centre. Sargon chastised the rebels. In 715 B.C. Rabshakeh (the title of the officer sent by Sennacherib) reproached Hezekiah: "Thou trustest upon the staff of this bruised reed, upon Egypt; whereupon if a man lean, it will go into his hand, and pierce it: So is Pharaoh King of Egypt unto all that trust on him" (2 Kings xviii. 21).

701 B.C.—Gaza remained subject to Sennacherib, the Assyrian king. Sennacherib died in 681 B.C. Tirhakah, the last king but one of the twenty-fifth (Ethiopian) dynasty, began to reign in 691 B.C. (2 Kings xix. 9).

674 B.C.—Esar-haddon, son of Sennacherib, one of the greatest Assyrian kings, retained Gaza (2 Kings xix. 37).

662 B.C.—One of Asshûr-bani-pal, King of Assyria's expeditions enveloped the east coast of the Mediterranean, including Gaza, which rendered him submission.

609 B.C.—Pharaoh Necho II took Gaza by force after the fall of the Empire of the Sargonides (Jeremiah xlvii. 1).

The Hellenistic population after this period became more numerous.

"The eight days' march across the sands from the Delta requires that, if an army came up that way into

Syria, Gaza, being their first relief from the desert, should be in friendly hands. Hence the continual efforts of Egypt to hold the town."—*G. A. Smith.*

624–596 B.C.—After some three generations of the dominion of Babylonia, Egypt once more spread its power. The sturdy Psamtek I (Psammetichus, "the lion's son") had, from 624–596, held the south of Palestine, including Gaza.

529 B.C.—Cambyses (Ahasuerus) King of Persians and Medes, after the fall of Babylon, set out for the conquest of Egypt. Gaza alone dared to resist him, and was not subdued till after a very long siege. There seems, however, to be considerable doubt as to Cambyses, the son of Cyrus. Xerxes is certainly the Ahasuerus of Ezra iv. 6, and of the Book of Esther.

332 B.C.—"Gaza was strong enough to resist for two months a seige of Alexander the Great, during which he was wounded. It was ultimately taken by storm, but not entirely destroyed. Bates, the Persian, who defended the city against Alexander, employed Arab mercenaries."—*G. A. Smith.*

All the maritime towns, save Tyre and Gaza, appear to have welcomed Alexander the Great and accepted his policy.

Gaza, next to Tyre, was the most important fortress in the Philistinian-Phœnician coast. Plutarch (*c.* A.D. 66), telling the story of its siege by Alexander, calls it "the biggest city of Syria."

After this siege, Gaza became more and more a Greek centre. New colonists settled within the city, which ceased to be a Philistine centre. Josephus expressly designated it a *πόλις Ελληνίς*.

315 B.C.—Gaza was conquered by Antigonus, King of

Asia, having been wrested from Ptolemy I, Soter, of Egypt (323-285), who had seized Philistia and garrisoned Gaza in 320 B.C.

312 B.C.—The city fell again into the hands of Ptolemy I, in consequence of his victory over Demetrius, the son of Antigonus.

In the same year, however, he renounced the possession of Cœle-Syria, and on his retreat had the most important fortresses, Gaza among them, demolished.

240 B.C.—The sovereignty over these districts changed several times during the decades next following, till at length they were for a longer period in the possession of the Ptolemies.

218-217 B.C.—Gaza, like the rest of Syria, was temporarily in the possession of Antiochus III (the Great). He is mentioned in 1 Macc. viii. 6-8. Becoming engaged in a quarrel with Egypt, he made four successive expeditions from Antioch to that country, in each case passing down the coast of Syria, inflicting misery on its inhabitants.

198 B.C.—Cœle-Syria came permanently under the dominion of the Seleucidæ, through the victory of Antiochus the Great at Panias. Gaza was conquered after a difficult siege.

The sway of the Seleucidæ is evidenced by a silver coin of Demetrius I, Soter, 162-150 B.C., minted at Gaza.

161-143 B.C.—During the leadership and high-priesthood of Jonathan "the wary" (who sided with Antiochus VI, son of Alexander Balas, against the faithlessness of Demetrius I), he lost no time in bringing the entire territory between Gaza and Damascus into subjection, with the assistance of Jewish and Syrian troops. Jonathan's history is one of constant intrigue, and his successes were due to craft and duplicity, rather than to valour and wisdom.

Gaza only yielded after Jonathan had recourse to forcible measures. He compelled the citizens to give hostages, and took them with him to Jerusalem.

Gaza at this time had a Council of 500 members.

141 B.C.—Gaza, the last of the Philistine towns not conquered by the Jews, was taken by Simon III, Ethnarch and High Priest. He is described in 1 Maccabees ii. 65, as "A man of counsel." A beautiful picture of him is to be found in 1 Maccabees xiv. 4-16.

96 B.C.—Gaza fell into the hands of King Alexander Jannæus, the third son of Hyrcanus, high priest, and a prince of the Maccabean line. He took the city after a year's siege, though at last only through treachery. He gave the inhabitants up to the sword, and entirely demolished the city.

"It was not till 96 B.C. that Jews actually crossed her walls, but in that year the pent-up hatred of centuries burst in devastation upon her."—*G. A. Smith.*

65 B.C.—When Pompey the Great conquered Syria, Gaza obtained her freedom. He arranged that the Roman general, A. Gabinius, Governor of Syria, should divide Judæa into five parts. Gabinius rebuilt Gaza 57 B.C. which was once more securely inhabited, and allowed it to resume its ancient prosperity under the power of Rome.[1] The newly built "maritime" and free city began a "new era" from the time of Pompey. According to some few authorities the ancient city was then forsaken, and the new town built somewhat farther southwards, possibly close to its harbour.

[1] *Ant.*, XIV. iv. 4; *Bell. Jud.*, I. vii. 7.

30 B.C.—Augustus, when in Egypt, handed Gaza over to King Herod I, of Philistine origin, who placed over this "maritime city" his brother-in-law, the Idumean Costobar. In favour of his *Ascalon* descent are certain allusions of Herod I to that city. At the death of Herod the Great, Gaza, still called a "maritime city," was annexed once more by Augustus to the province of Syria.[1]

Two of the passes through the Judæan and the Samaritan hills were strongly fortified by Herod I, who also held the tolls at Gaza, for Arabia by Petra and for Egypt. Gaza is the outpost of Africa, and the door of Asia.

Section II (A.D. 41–1913)

A.D. 41–54.—During the reign of Claudius, Gaza is spoken of as an important city by the Spanish geographer Pomponius Mela, with whom agree Eusebius and St. Jerome.

A.D. 66.—During the government of the fourteenth and last Judæan Procurator, Gessius Florus, Gaza was burned by the rebellious Jews. This destruction could have been but temporary, for there exist coins of Gaza, struck in honour of Vespasian and following emperors, which show that the city was still a place of importance soon after the destruction of Jerusalem.

The independence of the city is proved by the fact that Gaza had then its own independent kalendar.

A.D. 129–130.—Special tokens of favour were bestowed upon Gaza by Hadrian. The twenty-two coins of Gaza (the new era), as described in detail by De Saulcy, *Numismatique de la Palestine*, pp. 215–18, refer

[1] *Bell. Jud.*, I. xx. 3, and II. vi. 3.

to Hadrian's residence within the city. Dr. Coles, of Haifa, possesses a large number of Hadrian's Gaza coins.

"In the second and third centuries Gaza became a prosperous centre of Greek commerce and culture. Her schools were good, but her temples were famous, circling round the Marneion. . . . The schools of Gaza in philosophy and rhetoric grew more and more distinguished. Students, it is said, left Athens to learn the Attic style in Philistia, and even Persia borrowed her teachers." —*G. A. Smith.*

c. A.D. 300–371.—St. Hilarion, the first hermit of Palestine, was born at Thabatha, five miles from Gaza. (The reader is referred to Chapter IX for the Life of St. Hilarion.)

A.D. 307.—Copies of the Holy Scriptures had escaped their general destruction under Diocletian's Edict, and were still in use at Gaza when persecution raged there in this year.

A.D. 308.—St. Sylvanus, Bishop of Gaza, and others were martyred on May 4, during the persecution of Maximianus I.

A.D. 330.—Asclepas, Bishop of Gaza, who was accused of being "secretly tainted with Arianism," was deserted by the majority of the devout clergy and laity, and deposed, A.D. 341, but afterwards he received full acquittal.

Asclepas was present at the first Œcumenical Council of Nicœa, A.D. 325.

c. A.D. 335.—Constantine the Great rewarded the inhabitants of Mayoumas, the port of Gaza, for their unanimous adoption of Christianity, by erecting their town into "the city of Constantia" (Κωνστάντεια). It seems that this emperor, finding the inland city authorities obdurately pagan, gave a separate Constitution to its sea-town, but Julian (A.D. 361–363) took these privileges away.

A.D. 361.—At Mayoumas, the port of Gaza, the whole population was enthusiastically devoted to the Christian Faith, whereas Gaza was remarkable for its intense hatred.

Julian the Apostate's accession, A.D. 361, was the signal for an intensified persecution. He made Constantia again tributary to Gaza, but on his death its independence was restored.

A.D. 386.—St. Jerome and St. Paula, as early Christian pilgrims, after travelling among the Egyptian hermits, visited Gaza before returning to Bethlehem.

c. A.D. 401.—Eight heathen temples were destroyed through the influence of the Empress Eudoxia. As late as the fourth century an idol named Marnas was worshipped in the city.

In the Roman Imperial period commencing 27 B.C., the chief deity of the city was Marnas, Lord of heaven and sun and moon, as his name (מר = Lord) implies. He was originally a Shemitic deity, being, however, more or less disguised in a Greek garment.

A.D. 406.—On Easter Day St. Porphyrius consecrated the Church of Gaza, named after the Empress Eudoxia.

St. Porphyrius, a Greek ecclesiastic, after living five years as a hermit in the Thebaid of Egypt, went with his disciple Marcus to Jerusalem, and finally became Bishop of Gaza.

(For further particulars about St. Porphyrius, see Chapter VII.)

A.D. 541.—At the Council of Gaza, Pelagius (the first Pope of that name, A.D. 555–560) then a deacon, and

Roman Legate at Constantinople, was sent by order of the Emperor Justinian I (the Great) with letters, ordering the deposition of Paul,[1] the twenty-ninth Patriarch of Alexandria, which was accordingly carried out. This local Council was attended by Ephraim, Patriarch of Antioch, Peter, Patriarch of Jerusalem, the Metropolitan of Ephesus, and some other Prelates. Zoilus succeeded Paul in the Throne of St. Mark.

The story of the fall of Paul is involved in much confusion. He was consecrated by St. Menas, Patriarch of Constantinople, this being the first instance of an Alexandrian Patriarch being consecrated from the Throne of Constantinople. He held his see for about two years, from A.D. 539–541.

A.D. 635.—Gaza fell into the hands of Abu-Bekr, the general of the first Khalif, Omar, after a decisive battle with the Byzantine army. It was one of the first points of attack during this invasion, and about this date the city became Muslim.

The city was regarded as an important place by the Muslims, because Hashim ibn Abd Manaf, Mohammed's grandfather was buried there. About this date we hear little more of Muslim Gaza, except as its being the birthplace of Mohammed ibn Idris ash-Shâfiy, the founder of a Muslim sect, and the Great Doctor of the Law.

About the end of the sixth century, or the beginning of the seventh, Robinson (*Biblical Researches in Palestine*, vol. ii, p. 42) states that "Gaza was visited by Antoninus Martyr, who describes it as splendid and

[1] Paul was a native of Tarsus. He became a monk or abbot of the famous Upper Egyptian Rule of Tabenna, founded by St. Pachomius, *c.* A.D. 340.

delicious; and its inhabitants as noble, liberal, and friendly to strangers."

A.D. 672.—Gaza was visited by a great earthquake.

A.D. 796.—The city was laid waste during a furious civil war among the various Arab tribes inhabiting the country.

During the many wars between the Muslim rulers of Egypt and Syria, which preceded the Crusades, Gaza again suffered greatly.

A.D. 867.—Bernard the Wise—a Breton monk—describes Gaza as "very rich in all things."

A.D. 1149.—Baldwin III built a fortress at Gaza, in order to cut off the approach to Ascalon from the south.

The defence of the castle was entrusted to the Knights Templars.

The great buildings of Palestine are not to be ascribed to the Jews (for they were not a great building people), but to the Byzantine and Crusading Christian epochs.

A.D. 1170.—The Crusading castle at Dârûm (Deir el Belâh), three hours south of Gaza, was unsuccessfully stormed by Saladin.

A.D. 1170.—On December 20, Saladin made a dash on Gaza, but did not get possession of the citadel. He entered the city, and killed several of the inhabitants.

A.D. 1177.—At this date there were many Knights Templars in Gaza.

A.D. 1187.—Gaza passed into the hands of Saladin, after the Battle of Hattin on July 5.

A.D. 1192.—During the Third Crusade King Richard destroyed the Castle of Dârûm at Whitsuntide.

The walls of Gaza were dismantled after Richard Cœur de Lion's peace with Saladin in 1193.

A.D. 1238.—Defeat of the Crusaders at Gaza.

A.D. 1239.—Muslims were surprised in the neighbourhood of Gaza by Theobald, Count of Champagne and King of Navarre.

A.D. 1242.—During May, the Knights Templars and their Muslim allies defeated the Egyptian army, who were driven back to Gaza.

A.D. 1244.—The Christian and Saracen armies were annihilated by the Kharezmians in the valley of Gaza.

A.D. 1250.—King Louis IX and the Mameluke Emirs released their prisoners at Gaza.

A.D. 1260.—A garrison was stationed in Gaza by the Turkish invaders.

A.D. 1332.—Sir John Maundeville, a native of St. Albans, speaks of Gaza as "a gay and rich city; and it is very fair, and full of people, and is but a little distance from the sea." Like other cities of old, it was, for fear of pirates, built at some distance, about two and a half miles, from the sea.

A.D. 1370.—The Franciscan friar, John of Naples, martyred at Gaza.

A.D. 1432.—Bertrandon de la Brocguière, a knight in the service of the Duke of Burgundy, speaks of pilgrims being harshly treated in Gaza.

A.D. 1516.—The Turks crushed the Mamelukes at Gaza. This victory opened Egypt to Selim I of Constantinople. Egypt thus became a Pashalik of the Turkish Empire, and remained so until its conquest by Napoleon Bonaparte in 1799, when its Jewish inhabitants fled from the city.

A.D. 1584.—Samaritans are known to have lived in Gaza at this date, and possessed a synagogue. Two large baths in the city belonged to them. One of them still bears the name of "the Bath of the Samaritans." In

1907 an inscription was found at Gaza with a Biblical text, in Samaritan characters. The writing is not ancient, and it is still in the possession of the Muslim finder. During the occupancy of the Pashas of Gaza, one of them (of the fourth family Rid wan) desired to procure the inn and bath belonging to the Samaritan community. The owner objected, and gave them to the Muslims for the benefit of the Great Mosque. The Pasha consequently was indignant, and hanged the Samaritan at the gate of the inn. From the end of the sixteenth century we hear nothing more of the Samaritans at Gaza. (For additional information see also Chapter VI.)

A.D. 1771.—Ali Bey, a slave, obtained great power in Egypt, and occupied Gaza.

A.D. 1796.—Arabs destroyed Gaza during a civil war.

A.D. 1799.—Napoleon Bonaparte took Gaza in February, having crossed the desert with about 13,000 men.

"Napoleon has emphasised the indispensableness of Gaza, whether in the invasion or the defence of the Nile valley."—*G. A. Smith.*

A.D. 1831.—Mohammed Ali, a native of Roumelia, attacked Gaza in November, without being resisted.

A.D. 1839.—A great plague broke out in Gaza, and carried off large numbers of its inhabitants.

A.D. 1878.—The Church Missionary Society commenced work at Gaza.

CHAPTER III

FRANKINCENSE (ARABIAN) AND GAZA

In early times the Beduins of the desert were glad of a market in Gaza for their spices and frankincense.

In fact, according to Dr. Meyer (from whom I freely quote), the foundation of Gaza is most probably associated with the Minæans in their development of the frankincense trade. Extensive remains have been found in Central and Southern Arabia, which have been ascribed to these Minæans. Mr. Edward Glaser maintains that this people existed from about the seventeenth century B.C., and that the Sabæans followed them in the occupancy of those regions. If this be allowed, it seems to follow that Gaza was founded, or at least augmented, by this early Arabian people.

The wealth of the Minæan kingdom was derived chiefly from the transportation of frankincense and other spices from the East, and from Southern Arabia, which the caravans carried through the desert to Gaza.[1]

In 674 B.C. Esar-haddon, son of Sennacherib, undertook a campaign against the Arabian tribes, put an end to the Minæan kingdom, and secured control of the spice-trade route.

During the Persian period (539–332 B.C.) Gaza was the chief centre of the frankincense trade.

According to Dr. Birdwood in his article on "The Perfumes of the Bible," *Bible Educator*, vol. i, p. 378, "it is very surprising that so great a weight of evidence in favour of frankincense being produced in Arabia and Africa should ever have been set aside for the idle fancy that India was the source of the olibanum (ὁ λίβανος) of commerce."

[1] See Isaiah lx. 6, and Jeremiah vi. 20.

CHAPTER IV

NOTES ON GAZA COINS

An article of mine, entitled, "Notes on Gaza Coins," appeared in the *Quarterly Statement* of the Palestine Exploration Fund, April 1912. Since that date my attention has been drawn to an additional coin referred to by Dr. Meyer in his *History of the City of Gaza*, Chap. XVI. He begins by mentioning that an early coin attributed to Gaza is the so-called Jehovah coin of the British Museum. This coin is found in the printed catalogue of 1814, although purchased about fifty years previous. On palæographical and archæological grounds it is assigned to about 400 B.C. On the obverse appears a head with a helmet; on the reverse, a figure seated in a chariot, with a bird in his hand. Above the figure, in Phœnician characters, are the three letters יהו (YHW). A bearded head, wearing a mask, is also to be found on the reverse.

The coinage of Gaza in the fifth and fourth centuries B.C. has been identified by M. Six, and consists of darics and smaller coins of Attic weight and of various types.

In Nehemiah vii. 70, the Revised Version of the Old Testament reads thus: "The Tirshatha gave to the treasury a thousand darics of gold," whereas the Authorised Version has "a thousand drams of gold."

The gold daric and siglos (silver shekel) are the first coins that can possibly have had legal currency in Palestine.

In the second half of the fifth century B.C., the wealthy commercial cities on the Mediterranean seaboard had begun to issue silver money under their native kings. The great maritime city of Gaza was among the principal trade centres of this period.

Herodotus, *c.* 484–409 B.C. (iii. 5), mentions Gaza as scarcely inferior in size to Sardes, the capital of the kingdom of Lydia.

The influence of Athens at this date is strikingly shown by the coins of Gaza, which not only imitate the type and legend of the coins of Athens, but are struck on the Attic standard.

On March 20, 1912, at a meeting of the British Academy, in the rooms of the Royal Society, Mr. G. F. Hill, of the British Museum, read a paper on "Some Cults of Palestine in the Græco-Roman Age," from which the following passage is extracted—

"The coinage of Gaza entirely confirms and amplifies the evidence which has of late been accumulating concerning the primitive connection of the Philistine cities with Crete. The name of the great Gazaean god Marnas, who offered such stubborn resistance to Christianity, is probably not Syrian but Cretan. He is the Cretan Zeus, a young god, with a goddess resembling the huntress Artemis for his consort, just as in Crete there seems to be a connection between the young Zeus Velchanos and the goddess Britomartis, who is Artemis. Gaza was a Minoan foundation, and Minos—himself a form of the Cretan Zeus—was worshipped at Gaza, which, indeed, was actually called Minoa." [1]

After the capture of Gaza by Alexander the Great, 332 B.C., regal coins were struck there with the frequent

[1] On some coins the word ΜΕΙΝΩ occurs. It refers to Minoa, the legendary name of Gaza, with reference to its foundation by Minos of Crete.—*Meyer*.

monogram $\overline{\Gamma A}$, both under Ptolemy II, Philadelphus, 285–246 B.C., Ptolemy III, Euergetes I, 246–221 B.C., and Demetrius I, Soter, of Syria, 162–150 B.C.

The autonomous bronze money of Gaza dates from an era commencing 61 B.C. Of this period no silver money of Gaza is extant.

The imperial coins of Gaza from Augustus to Gordian bear two different sets of dates; the first Gaza era beginning 61 B.C., the second beginning A.D. 129. The second era probably commemorates the visit of Hadrian to Gaza.[1] On some of the coins these two eras appear concurrent. These imperial coins, with inscriptions ΓΑΖΑΙΩΝ, ΓΑΖΑ, etc., have usually the addition of the Phœnician letter 𐤌, from which the Swastica, the characteristic mark on Gaza coins, is possibly derived, the initial representing the divinity Marnas. The Temple of Marnas was called the Marneion.[2]

"In the last days of paganism the great god of Gaza, now known as Marnas (our lord), was regarded as the god of rains, and invoked against famine. That Marnas was lineally descended from Dagon is probable, and it is therefore interesting to note that he gave oracles, that he had a circular temple, where he was sometimes worshipped by human sacrifices, that there were wells in the sacred circuit, and that there was also a place of adoration to him, situated, in old Semitic fashion, outside the town. Certain *Marmora* in the temple, which might not be approached, especially by women, may perhaps be

[1] Hadrianus, A.D. 117–138, favoured Gaza with several visits from A.D 123–135. This probably accounts for De Saulcy (*Numismatique de la Terre Sainte*, Paris, 1874) being able to describe, on pp. 215–18, twenty-two Gaza coins of this reign.

[2] *Historia Numorum*, Head, p. 680.

connected with the threshold which the priests of Dagon would not touch with their feet "[1] (1 Sam. v. 5).

Herod Agrippa I became King of Judæa A.D. 41, and possessed the entire kingdom of Herod the Great. Among the coins of Agrippa I under Claudius, Madden (*Coins of the Jews*, p. 137, No. 2) reproduces a coin which probably represents a ceremony taking place in the temple of the god Marnas at Gaza. "There were in Gaza eight temples of the Sun, of Venus, of Apollo, of Proserpine, and of Hecate; that which is called Heroon, or of the Priests, that of the Fortune of the City, called Τυχεῖον, and that of Marneion, which the citizens said is the Cretan-born Jupiter, and which they considered to be more glorious than any other temple in existence."

Dr. Donald Coles, of Haifa, has, in his collection of over one hundred specimens of Gaza coins, an exceptionally interesting coin of Hadrian, A.D. 130, in excellent condition, re-struck under Simon Bar-Cochab, A.D. 132–135. This Hadrian bronze coin is quoted in De Saulcy's *Numismatique de la Terre Sainte*, p. 215, No. 1, and the re-struck coin during the Revolt of the Jews, A.D. 132–135 is reproduced on Plate XV, No. 4, in his *Recherches sur la numismatique judaique*.

It was not unusual for these Simon Bar-Cochab coins to be re-struck from Ascalon, and other current coinage.

Among all the writers in the *Quarterly Statement* of the P. E. F. from 1894–1901 on the Swastica, or Fylfot, not one of them seems to be aware that the Swastica is constantly found as the distinguishing mint-mark of Gaza, *e.g.* on Plate XI of *Numismatique de la Palestine*, Gaza coins, there are both the sign 卐 of the male Swas-

[1] *Encyclopædia Britannica*, "Philistines," pp. 755–6, vol. xviii, ninth edition.

tica, and the more common 卍 female Swastica, revolving in the opposite direction on the reverse of coins of Hadrian, Antoninus Pius, Lucius Verus, Faustina Junior and Lucilla, Julia Domna, Plautilla, Geta.

The Swastica is an Eastern symbol of the Sun, and is occasionally known as Gammadion, and mystic Fylfot. The latest idea formed regarding the Swastica is, that it may be a form of the old wheel symbolism, and that it represents the solar system. It is often connected with the Sun, as in the Island of Melos, first colonised by Phœnicia. Its great diffusion in Eastern Asia is due to its being a Buddhist emblem, "the wheel of the law."

In the Catacombs at Rome it is well known on the tunic of the Good Shepherd, and on the garments of the Fossores, a class of men employed in the offices of Christian sepulture, and in opening fresh graves and catacombs.

The Triskelia, or Three Legs of the Isle of Man, and some Syracuse coins in the reign of Agathocles, 317–289 B.C., and other towns in Sicily, are only variants of the Swastica.

Dr. Albert Churchward, in *The Signs and Symbols of Primordial Man* (London: Swan, Sonnenschein & Co., Ltd., 1910), supplies a mint of valuable information scattered throughout this learned work. On page 44 he states that this Swastica was also the most sacred sign amongst the British Druids. Page 115 (figure 49) shows the Mexican Kalendar in form of a Swastica Cross. On page 261 the Swastica is said to be frequently found on stones in Devonshire, and a good specimen is in the museum at Torquay.

"It is a fact that prehistoric man of the two hemispheres had the knowledge to spin fibre and thread, to wind it on bobbins (see spindle wheels found in museums) having the same sign on them wherever found, viz. the Swastika 卍" (p. 44).

"This symbol has probably a wider range than any other that has been preserved from prehistoric times" (p. 352).

Dr. Churchward states, in *Primordial Man*, p. 187, that the recent discoveries of Flinders Petrie at Abydos tend to show that the Druids derived the Swastika from Egypt more than 20,000 years ago!!!

On April 16, 1912, a few poor specimens of Roman bronze coins struck at Gaza were brought to me in that city, but the local finds seem to have become nearly exhausted.

A representation of the temple Tychæon erected to the Fortune of the City occurs on a coin of Antoninus and Marcus Aurelius (shortly before A.D. 161), which shows a tetrastyle temple. (Most of the temples depicted on the Gaza coins are distyle.) The goddess of the town, as well as the heifer, also appear on this coin.

CHAPTER V

THE JEWS AT GAZA [1]

THERE is no record to show that the Jews obtained any stronghold in Gaza during Pagan times.

Pompey liberated Gaza *c.* 65 B.C., which had been subjected to the Jews since the times of the Maccabees, and restored the city to its freedom.

[1] It will be noticed that this chapter does not refer to the earliest connections of Jews with Gaza.

With the institutions of Pompey, the freedom of the Jewish people, after having existed for scarcely eighty years, if we reckon it as beginning in 142 B.C., was completely overthrown.

Josephus says (*The Jewish War*, II. 18, 1) that after the people of Cæsarea had slain about 20,000 Jews, and all the city was emptied of its Jewish inhabitants, A.D. 66, the whole nation was greatly enraged, so the Jews divided themselves into parties, utterly demolishing Anthedon and Gaza.

Schürer (*History of the Jewish People in the Time of Christ*, II. vol. i, p. 71), however, thinks that this must have been a very partial destruction, for so strong a fortress as Gaza could not have been actually destroyed by a band of insurrectionary Jews.

During the middle ages, the use of wine being forbidden to Muslims by the Kûrân, it was manufactured in Gaza only by the Jews. This Jewish wine trade remained in their hands exclusively for a lengthened period. There was also a colony of wine-dealers in the harbour Mayoumas.

In February 1799 most of the Jews fled when the French troops under Napoleon entered Gaza. Meyer says that in 1811 there were none left. Their synagogue stood idle, and their cemetery was deserted.

There were supposed to be, in 1907, about one hundred and sixty Jews in Gaza (of whom thirty were Sephardim).

CHAPTER VI

THE SAMARITANS

Meyer supplies some valuable information about the Samaritans in Gaza on pages 71–2, from which I gratefully cull a few sentences. He writes of their having settled there early, maintaining themselves as a separate community till the modern period. A complete history is impossible, because of the meagreness of the record. It is remarkable how this little sect spread all over Palestine, and even into Egypt. There are records of the Samaritans at Gaza from the fourth to the seventeenth centuries. According to the Samaritan Chronicle of the High Priest Eleazar, the territory of Palestine, and other parts of Syria and Egypt, were assigned to various Samaritan families at the time of Baba the Great (end of fourth century). That extending from Gaza to the River of Egypt was given to Israel ben Machir, and Shalum was assigned to it as Priest; the territory from Carmel to Gaza to Laib ben Becher, with Joseph as its Priest. All the Samaritans who settled at Gaza were of the tribe of Benjamin, excepting Mouzaf ben Mitpalel of the tribe of Ephraim. The Martyr Paul of Gaza, *c.* A.D. 300, before his death at Cæsarea, prayed for the Samaritans of his native town.

During the reign of Justinian, *c.* A.D. 529, the imperial troops once occupied the city on the occasion of an uprising of the Samaritan inhabitants of the district, and the citizens were greatly disturbed. The Bishop Marcianus stepped into the breach, and settled the affair by organising a militia to which the matters in dispute were referred. The imperial troops were withdrawn, and peace was restored.

There were many Samaritans at Gaza in the seventh century. After the Muslim conquest, A.D. 634, the Samaritans of Gaza deposited their property with their high priest, and fled to the east.

The five hundred Samaritans who had been captured at Shechem by Bazawash, governor of Demascus, *c.* A.D. 1137, were redeemed by a co-religionist of Acre. Many of these settled in Gaza.

In A.D. 1674 the Samaritans living at Gaza addressed a letter to Robert Huntington, who was deeply interested in their religion and literature.

Clermont-Ganneau reports the finding of a Samaritan liturgical inscription at Gaza, but does not produce it either in the original or in translation. Able also reports a fragment of a decalogue in the Samaritan script of the Mohammedan period.

Among the *Gleanings from the Minute Books* of the Jerusalem Literature Society, November 1849, Mr. E. T. Rogers remarks that the Samaritans are still quite a distinct set of people, as they were in the time of our Saviour. They make no proselytes; never intermarry with people of other sects, and are particularly clean as a people; none others are known than those now in Nablus. Their principal distinction in the oriental crowd is that they wear a crimson turban.

When the Rev. Dr. E. H. Thomson visited Nablus, in May 1898, he asked after the fate of the Samaritan community that was still surviving in Gaza when Baron Sylvestre de Sacy, *c.* 1829, corresponded with the Samaritans of Nablus. He was informed that the community in Gaza had ceased to exist some sixty years before. Now, at all events, these one hundred and sixty Samaritans resident in Nablus are all that remain of the Samaritan race and creed.

Mr. J. G. Pickard, writing from Gaza in *The Quarterly Statement* P. E. F., July 1873, reports on the newly discovered Samaritan Stone of which the inscription is a passage in Deuteronomy iv. 29–31. It has been suggested that this stone belonged to a Samaritan synagogue in Gaza. The spot where the stone was discovered is about a mile and a half from the sea shore.

CHAPTER VII

SOME EARLY BISHOPS OF (I) GAZA, (II) MAYOUMAS (THE PORT OF GAZA)

Palestina Prima—Cæsarea, ***Metropolis.***

The Dictionary of Christian Antiquities, p. 1631, mentions "Philemon (1) Bishop of Gaza; commemorated February 14 (Basil Menol)."

The Kalendar of the Byzantine Church, on November 22, commemorates "Philemon, Apostle."

The Jerusalem Archimandrite Meletius Metaxakis, (now Bishop of Kition, Cyprus), in an article on the Madaba Mosaic Map, *Nea Sion*, May and June 1907, p. 485, states that "according to *The Ecclesiastical Treatise about the Seventy Disciples of the Lord*, Philemon, the Apostle, to whom the Epistle of Paul is directed, became Bishop of Gaza."

The legendary history of Philemon supplies nothing on which we can rely. *The Apostolic Constitutions* (vii. 46) relate that Philemon became Bishop of Colosse, and died a martyr under Nero, but this is not sustained by any other early testimony, and is expressly denied by the author of the *Commentary on St. Paul's Epistles*, attributed to Hillary. This tradition, therefore, which Dr. Meyer (p. 59) mentions, apparently without hesitation, cannot, I think, be accepted.

I.—Bishops of Gaza

c. A.D. 285. Sylvanus. The first Christian martyr of Gaza whose name is known. Having had his eyes put out, he was beheaded at the Copper Mines of Phæno.

Commemorated May 4.

A.D. 325. Gaza was represented by a Bishop at the Council of Nicæa. He is described as a Bishop "of *the Churches round Gaza.*"

A.D. 341. Asclepas.[1] His name occurs in the Minutes of the First Œcumenical Council. He succeeded Sylvanus, but was deposed at a Council of Antioch, and reinstated at a Council of Sardica.

He suffered many persecutions for the "Orthodox" faith.

A.D. 341. Quintianus, an Arian usurper of the See of Asclepas.

A.D. 363. Irenæus (A.D. 363–393) was present at the Council of Antioch A.D. 363. He built the Church of St. Irene in Gaza. The first church built in Gaza itself was the work of St. Irenæus, who died *c.* A.D. 393, and whose feast is December 16.

A.D. 393. Aeneias succeeded Irenæus. His episcopate lasted for a very short period.

A.D. 395. Porphyrius, the true restorer of Christianity in Gaza. His life was written by his trusty

[1] Also called Asclepius. He was on the side of St. Athanasius.

deacon, Marcus. The text was published at Leipsig in 1895. Porphyrius was born in Thessalonica, *c.* A.D. 347, of a good family. After a Presbyterate of three years, in A.D. 395 he was unwillingly consecrated Bishop of Gaza by John of Cæsarea.

"Porphyry sent Marcus to Constantinople, and obtained from the Emperor a Decree closing the Temples of Gaza; Cynegius came to the city with Christian police from Ascalon; the temples were closed, and the consultation of their oracles was forbidden. Idolatry did not cease, however; the oracles were still consulted, though surreptitiously, for permitting which Cynegius was said to have received a large amount of gold. The Christians were still persecuted, and Porphyrius therefore determined on further measures. He went to Cæsarea, consulted with the Archbishop John, and both of them set out for Constantinople in A.D. 401. Through the offices of Amantius, the Chamberlain, they were presented to the Empress Eudoxia. They prophesied for her the birth of a son; and the Empress vowed a church for Gaza, if the prophecy should be fulfilled. The promised son, Theodosius the younger, was born; and, true to her word, Eudoxia interceded with the Emperor for a rescript closing the Gazæan temples. For reasons of State, the Emperor hesitated to grant the request: 'though the city is idolatrous, it is peaceful and pays its taxes regularly. If it is disturbed, it is to be feared that its inhabitants would desert it, and its trade be ruined.' He therefore suggested mild means for winning the city to Christianity. The rescript was obtained from the Emperor at the baptism of his infant son, being issued as the first decree of the new prince. Before the Bishops left Constantinople, Eudoxia provided them with funds for building a church and a hospice in Gaza; and the Emperor added gifts on his own account."[1]

St. Chrysostom was *then* high in the Empress's favour.

St. Porphyrius is said to have been indefatigable in instructing the people of Gaza in a simple and popular style, based entirely on Holy Scripture. He was present at the Council of Diospolis, A.D. 415.

On one occasion, owing to a terrible drought at Gaza, the Christians prayed with fervour to Almighty God for rain. The amount of rain which fell in response gave St. Porphyrius much influence over the heathen, and numbers of them were baptised. He died A.D. 420.

His name is commemorated, in the Byzantine Church Kalendar, on February 26.

A.D. 449. NATORIS was present at the Council of Ephesus, A.D. 431, and was consecrated *c.* A.D. 449. At the Council of Ephesus he supported Juvenal, Bishop of Jerusalem, who was accused of irregularities of ecclesiastical practice.

TIMOTHEUS, during the reign of Anastasius I, A.D. 430–513.

A.D. 490. ENOS (ÆNAS), who had been a Platonic philosopher, and convert to Christianity, testifies to certain persons speaking after the loss of their tongues (See Robertson's *Church History*, p. 459, *note*).

A.D. 518. KYRILLUS, who condemned Severus of Antioch.

A.D. 540. MARCIANUS (reign of Justinius, A.D. 483–565).

He built two churches in the city, the church of St. Sergius, and that of St. Stephen, whose beauty is praised by Chorikius of Gaza.

[1] Meyer's *History of the City of Gaza*, p. 64.

A.D. 540. AURELIANUS, a successor, perhaps, of Marcianus.

A.D. 553. The Bishops of Gaza and Mayoumas Gazæ each signed synodical letters inserted in the Acts of the Second Council of Constantinople.[1]

II.—BISHOPS OF MAYOUMAS (OR CONSTANTIA)[2]

c. A.D. 400. ZENO, brother of Aias, the Bishop of Botolion (Bethulia), and personally known to the historian Sozimus.

A.D. 431. PAULINUS, mentioned in the Minutes of the Council of Ephesus.

A.D. 449. PAULUS, the supporter of Dioscorus in the Robber Council of Ephesus, A.D. 449.

A.D. 505. PETER, the Iberian, Bishop of Gaza and

[1] "Till A.D. 536 the names of the Bishops of Gaza were preserved in the records of the Council of Jerusalem" (Meyer, p. 67).

According to Meyer, p. 69, from the sixth to the twelfth centuries, Gaza was an Episcopal See of the Latin Church.

In the sixth century, reference is made by Theodosius to a Bishop Suffragan of Gaza.

The Archimandrite Metaxakis states that in the Kalendar of the Abyssinian Saints there is a Feast of St. John, Bishop of Gaza, on April 6, but the Ethiopic Kalendar, according to Neale (*History of the Holy Eastern Church*, vol. ii), does not include this name.

Conder (*Quarterly Statement* P. E. F., July 1875, p. 10), asserts that the Bishop of Gaza bears the additional title of Mâr Jîryîs to the present day. Sophronius is the titular Archbishop of Gaza in 1913. He is non-resident.

[2] Of Mayoumas, or Constantia (so called from the son of Constantine), a city independent of Gaza, which from the time of Constantine the Great formed an episcopal see, six Bishops are named (*Nea Sion*, May and June 1907, p. 491). The name Mayoumas does not appear till Christian times. Keith explored the site in 1844, and found widespread traces of an extinct city.

Mayoumas. An Eutychian, appointed by the Alexandrian faction.

During this Episcopate, Severus, the Monophysite Patriarch of Antioch, had been expelled from a convent lying between Gaza and Mayoumas as an heretical blasphemer. Coming to the Emperor Anastasius Dicorus, who was infected with the same heresy, he was appointed a noble, and by the use of flatteries, and false accusations, he advanced so far that by the command of Dicorus he banished the Patriarch of Antioch, Flavian II, from the throne, sent him into exile to Petra, and ascended the throne by violence. He excited a great tumult in Antioch.[1]

A.D. 516. PROCOPIUS. His signature appears in the Letter of John of Jerusalem.

A.D. 700–760. ST. COSMAS, Hymnologist, surnamed Μελῳδός. He acquired the appellation of Hagiopolites, on account of his proficiency in polite literature. Having been captured by the Saracens, he was carried to Damascus, and had the honour to be preceptor of St. John Damascene, his foster-brother.

St. Cosmas, like his friend, St. John Damascene, became a monk of St. Sabas, and against his will was consecrated Bishop of Mayoumas, by John, Patriarch of Jerusalem, the same who ordained St. John Damascene, priest. Dr. Neale considers him the most learned of Greek Church poets. After ministering his diocese with great holiness, he departed this life in a good old age, and is commemorated on October 14.

[1] Neale's *The Patriarchate of Antioch*, pp. 163–4.

CHAPTER VIII

THIRTEEN MARTYRS AT GAZA

A.D. 304. TIMOTHEUS suffered martyrdom under Urban, the prefect of the province, in the second year of Diocletian's persecution.

A.D. 304. The Syriac version of the history of the martyrs in Palestine states that THECLA with AGAPIUS was cast to the wild beasts in the year of Timotheus' martyrdom.

c. A.D. 308. SYLVANUS, Bishop of Gaza, was a martyr in the persecution of Maximianus I. He was a Presbyter at the outbreak, and from the beginning he endured much suffering with fortitude. Shortly before his martyrdom, which was among the last in Palestine at that period, he obtained the Episcopate.

Eusebius speaks with admiration of his Christian endurance, saying he was "reserved until that time, that this might be the last seal of the whole conflict in Palestine."

This aged martyr was eminent for his confessions from the very first day of the persecution. In early manhood he had served as a soldier, before receiving Holy Orders.

Dr. Meyer (*History of the City of Gaza*, p. 60. New York, 1907) states that "the first Christian martyr of Gaza whose name is known is the Bishop Sylvanus, who met his death in 285." Eusebius (*Ecclesiastical History*, Book VIII, Chap. XIII), however, remarks that Sylvanus was "beheaded with thirty-nine others at the Copper Mines of Phœne." Early Christians of Gaza were not infrequently martyred at headquarters in Cæsarea (Palestinæ).

A.D. 308. JOHN, a student of Holy Writ and of wonderful memory, was associated with Sylvanus. He endured many tortures and was decapitated with his Bishop.

A.D. 308. HATHA (ST. THEA), a virgin of Gaza, suffered martyrdom under Firmilian in Cæsarea.

A.D. 361. During the reign of Julian, the pagans of Gaza attempted to destroy the church built by St. Hilarion. During this revolt, Eusebius, a Gaza Christian, with his brothers Nestabis and Zeno, were thrown into prison, beheaded, and their bodies were burned outside the city walls, on a spot used for the disposal of dead animals.

This persecution induced all the Christians to leave Gaza. The case was brought to the attention of the Emperor. It seems that the heathen governor of Gaza had imprisoned the citizens who had abused the Christians, whereupon Julian exiled him.

About the same date, Nestor—a Confessor (according to the Rev. S. Baring-Gould, *Lives of the Saints*)—was killed of wounds inflicted by the populace.

A.D. 1370. The Franciscan Chronicles of the fourteenth century relate that a Franciscan friar, John of Naples, went from Jerusalem to Gaza, and was subjected to a cruel martyrdom.

A.D. 1555. Two French pilgrims were arrested at Gaza, and on their refusing to renounce the religion of CHRIST were put to death. Their bodies, carried away by the Christians, were buried under Orthodox Greek auspices.[1]

[1] *New Guide to the Holy Land*, p. 534. The Church recognises many Gaza saints, *e. g.* Dorotheus, Dositheus, Barsanuphius, and John the Prophet.

CHAPTER IX

ST. HILARION, THE FIRST HERMIT OF PALESTINE (c. A.D. 290–371).

"THE solitary life never found so many votaries in Europe as in Egypt and Palestine. Partly because of the comparative inclemency of the climate, and the proportionate need of more appliances to support life, and partly because of the more practical character of the West. As might be expected, for obvious reasons there have been fewer female hermits" (*Dictionary of Christian Antiquities:* Article HERMITS, 1875).

During the third century, Eremites (from ἐρῆμος, desert), or *Hermits*, retired entirely from the haunts of men, and buried themselves in the wildest and most inaccessible solitudes.

In Palestine, the hermit life was introduced by St. Hilarion, a disciple of St. Antony.

The first Palestinian convent was founded by St. Hilarion, A.D. 328. He was pre-eminently a teacher. Every novice was given a special occupation.

Hilarion was born at Thabatha, a village five miles to the south of Gaza, c. A.D. 290, of heathen parents, who sent him to Alexandria for education. There he showed proficiency in rhetoric. He became a Christian, and turning from the attractions of the circus and theatre, spent all his leisure in attending Church services.

The monastic retreat of St. Antony, the founder of Asceticism, attracted Hilarion, and he became his enthusiastic disciple for two months.

Next neighbours to the Church of Egypt, the early

Christians of Gaza naturally imitated the asceticism of Antony, and avowed the orthodoxy of Athanasius. Hilarion found, however, that his mountain retreat was too much thronged with followers to suit his taste. At the age of fifteen years he therefore decided to become a hermit. He returned to Palestine, and finding his parents dead, he gave away all his goods, and went to live in a desert spot seven miles from the Christian city of Mayoumas.

The boy hermit was clad in a sackcloth shirt, which he never changed till it was worn out, a cloak of skins which Antony had given him, and a blanket, such as peasants wore.

His earliest diet was a daily fast until sunset, and then a supper of fifteen figs. His employment was basket-making, after the fashion of the Egyptian monks. His dwelling was so small as rather to resemble a tomb. He had resided in the desert twenty-two years when he first became celebrated for his miracles.

The first miracle of healing with which St. Hilarion is credited was the restoration to health of three children at Gaza, whose mother had induced him to come forth from his retreat to see them. Standing beside their bed, the hermit merely uttered the word "Jesus," and they at once recovered. On his return to his cell he was so besieged by other applicants for relief that he could no longer lead his sécluded life.[1]

In his sixty-third year, hearing of the decease of St. Antony, St. Hilarion resolved to visit the place where the great recluse had entered into rest, hoping thus to escape from the crowds by whom he was now constantly sur-

[1] For the Miracles of St. Hilarion see Neale's *Patriarchate of Antioch*, pp. 111–13.

rounded. Resisting all the efforts of the Egyptian hermits to become their leader, he returned alone to Gaza, but no sooner had he left them than messengers arrived with orders from Julian the Apostate to slay Hilarion, and his disciple Hesychius, wherever they should be found.

During Hilarion's absence in Egypt, the heathen citizens of Gaza destroyed his monastery at Mayoumas.

During his life of fifty years in Palestine, he visited the holy sites but once, and for a single day—in order, as he said, that he might neither appear to despise them on account of their meanness, nor to suppose that GOD's grace was limited to any particular place. During, apparently, this short visit to Jerusalem, a pleasing story is told of him in connection with his friend St. Epiphanius, Archbishop of Constantia (formerly Salamís) and Metropolitan of Cyprus. Hilarion called upon this Bishop. Some fowls were served up at the table, and St. Epiphanius asked his guest to partake of them. Hilarion excused himself, saying that, since he put on the habit of a recluse, he had never eaten of any animal. "And I," said Epiphanius, "since I put on the same habit, have never allowed that any one should lie down to sleep with a grievance against me on his mind, even as I have never gone to rest at variance with any one." "Father," replied the hermit, "your rule is more excellent than mine."

For additional information concerning the celebrated St. Epiphanius, A.D. 368–404, and his intimate connection with St. Hilarion, see Hackett's *History of the Orthodox Church of Cyprus*, pp. 399–407, *etc.*

"Our Father and Archbishop Epiphanius of Cyprus" is commemorated in the Byzantine Kalendar on May 12.

At last, in a wilderness near Paphos in Cyprus, death

released Hilarion, this much persecuted saint, from importunities. Almost with his last breath he expressed a wish as to where his body was to be buried—without pomp or ceremony. His wishes were respected, but his friend and favourite disciple, Hesychius, stole his body from the grave, re-interring it in his own monastery at Mayoumas. A rivalry ensued between the places of the first and second interments; miracles were said to be performed at both.

According to Sozomen, his festival was observed in Palestine with great solemnity as early as the fifth century.

St. Hilarion's name occurs in the Byzantine Kalendar on October 21, as

"Our Father Hilarion the Great."[1]

CHAPTER X

SOZOMEN, CHURCH HISTORIAN (A.D. 400–c. 450)

Salamanes Hermias Sozomenus, called Scholasticus, came of a wealthy family, and was born at Bethelia, a small town close to Gaza, c. A.D. 400, where his grandfather had been one of the first to embrace Christianity, probably under Constantius, through the influence of St. Hilarion. This hermit, among his other miracles, had miraculously healed an acquaintance of Sozomen's grandfather, one Alaphion. Both men, with their families, became zealous Christians, and were conspicuous for their virtues. Having been endowed with great

[1] For the chariot race during the life of Hilarion see Appendix I, on the Circus of Gaza.

natural ability, this ancestor of Sozomen was distinguished as an interpreter of Holy Scripture, and held fast his Christian profession, even in the time of Julian. Sozomen was educated at first in Bethelia, among the monks, for some memories of his youth are connected with the neighbourhood of Gaza. In early manhood he went to Berytus (Beirût) [1] to be trained in civil law at its famous school. As a man he retained the impressions of his youth. When he became an Advocate of Constantinople, he wrote his chief work, Ἐκκλησιαστικὴ Ἱστορία. c. A.D. 440.—It consisted of nine books, from A.D. 323–423, a continuation of Eusebius. It is a monument of his reverence for the monks in general, and also for the disciples of St. Hilarion in particular. He dedicated it to the Emperor Theodosius II. What Sozomen has to tell of the history of Southern Palestine was derived from oral tradition. Sozomen died c. A.D. 450.

Bethelia was formerly a town with a famous heathen temple, renowned for its beauty and age, which Sozomen calls "the village of the Gazæans." It is now the Arabic Beit Lehia, which lies among the olive groves north of the city, and retains its religious character by the mosque and minaret which, no doubt, replaced the ancient temple.

[1] "Beirût" became renowned, during the Norman period, for its great law school, perhaps the most famous in the empire."—*The History of Beirût*, by Prof. Harvey Porter, Ph.D., pp. 30-1, 1912.

CHAPTER XI

THE ORTHODOX GREEK CHURCH IN GAZA

On April 17, 1912, an opportunity was afforded me of a lengthy conversation with the Archimandrite Antonius, who was educated at the convent of the Cross, Jerusalem, and the Greek College, Halki, Sea of Marmora. He has been in charge of the Orthodox Syrian congregation at Gaza during the last seven years.

I inquired as to the exact spot where St. Hilarion, the first hermit of Palestine, was buried. It seems that both Christians and Muslims reverence his grave at Deir-el-Belah (the ancient Ed-Dârûm), two hours' ride south of Gaza, where the mosque Jami el-Khidr stands on the site of an old chapel.

In the fourth century there were several hermits at Thabatha, one and a half hours' ride to the south of Gaza. During the fifth century the existence of three ancient city churches is recorded: Eudoxiana, Irene, and the Church of the Holy Apostles on the south. The two new churches were St. Sergius and St. Stephen the Protomartyr.

The Archimandrite stated that the dedication of his church was associated with the name of St. Porphyrius, and was built in A.D. 443. The grave of this early Gaza prelate is within the church, which was restored in 1866. There is an ancient circular marble font for immersion in the north-west of the nave.

The Patriarch Damianus on one occasion visited Gaza, but Sophronius, its titular Bishop, has never entered the city.

A native Arabic-speaking priest is associated with the Archimandrite. The services are rendered in Greek, although the Epistles and Gospels are said in Arabic. The whole of the congregation of one thousand "Orthodox" are only familiar with Arabic. The two Orthodox schools contain ninety boys and twenty-five girls. A friendly feeling exists between these Orthodox Christians and Muslims.

CHAPTER XII

(1) THE EMPRESS EUDOXIA.—(2) THE GAZA CHURCH "EUDOXIANA" [1]

1. THE Emperor Arcadius married Eudoxia, a beautiful Frank maiden, the daughter of Bauto, who had held office as master of the soldiery.

Arcadius, always weak and indolent, was accustomed to be ruled by his clever wife. "She imagined herself to be religious, because she was liberal in almsgiving, and in building churches, attended the Church services, reverenced the relics of martyrs, and patronised the clergy, so long as they let her have her own way. But she was superstitious, thoroughly worldly-minded, avaricious, absorbed in luxuries and pleasures, and these of a not very innocent character. She at first welcomed St. Chrysostom, and assured him of her favour, but soon turned against him." [2] Her death occurred on October 4, 404.

[1] Additional information concerning this church is contained in Mr. G. F. Hill's translation of *The Life of Porphyry by Mark the Deacon*. Oxford: the Clarendon Press, 1913. Unfortunately, my attention was only drawn to this charming little book after these pages were in the hands of the printer.

[2] Hore's *Eighteen Centuries of the Orthodox Greek Church*, p. 188. James Parker & Co., 1899.

2. At the end of the fourth century there were eight heathen temples within the city—that of the Sun, of Venus, of Apollo, of Koré (Proserpina), of Hecate, that known as the Heroon (Ἡρῷον), of Juno, of the City's fortune called the Tychæon (Τυχεῖον[1]) depicted on the coins of Gaza, and lastly that of Marnas, that is to say the Marneion, which was thought as being that of Zeus of Crete, and was held to be the most famous of all the temples. There were, besides, numberless idols in the houses and in the villages. A church was built on the site of the Marneion, which latter was destroyed by order of the Empress Eudoxia. The plans of the new church were sent from Constantinople, and were adapted by the architect Rufinus, of Antioch. The construction of the church took five years to complete. It was consecrated by Porphyrius on Easter Day, A.D. 406, and dedicated to St. John Baptist. The Deacon Mark (Biographer of Bishop Porphyrius) says that there were about one thousand hermits present at its consecration.

"The enforcement of Arcadius' Decree was entrusted to Cynegius, who arrived at Gaza ten days after Porphyrius with a force of soldiers and a body of civil officers. When the order for closing the temples was read, the citizens protested; but the soldiers carried out the Imperial commands, and were aided by the Christians and the sailors. The fiercest opposition was encountered at the Marneion, where the priests blocked the entrance with large stones. Seeing, however, that their defence was vain, they buried the temple treasures and escaped. The Marneion was then burned; it took ten days to complete the destruction of all the temples. After the site of the Marneion had been purified, a cruciform

[1] See page 44, under chapter on Coins.

church was built on it out of the funds furnished by Eudoxia, after whom it was named the 'Eudoxiana.'

"The courtyard of the church was paved with stones taken from the Marneion, and the women of Gaza refused to walk in it because of their strong attachment to the old cult."[1]

The Eudoxiana was eventually converted into a mosque, and the Roman garrison, consisting of sixty soldiers under the command of Callinicus, having refused to apostatise, were slain at Eleutheropolis and Jerusalem.

CHAPTER XIII

THE CRUSADERS AT GAZA (A.D. 1100–1291)

Of seven towns along the Palestine and Syrian coast Ascalon was brought into the most frequent contact with the Crusaders, and Gaza received the fewest visits. "The Crusaders alone do not appear to have used Gaza for commerce, because this city was never so securely in their hands as to permit them to dominate the roads south and east for any distance."—*G. A. Smith.*

A.D. 1100.—The Crusaders rebuilt the castle in the centre of the city, and from this date Ascalon was made of more importance by the Christians.

A.D. 1149.—The most renowned of the three great military orders founded in the twelfth century for the defence of the Latin kingdom of Jerusalem was that of the Knights Templars. From the first this order was strictly a military one. White mantles were worn with

[1] Meyer's *History of the City of Gaza*, pp. 64, 65.

a red cross. After Baldwin III returned from Antioch, towards the end of 1149, he was engaged in building a fortress at Gaza.

It was nearly completed in the spring of 1150, and was handed over to the Knights Templars.

Gaza was the last Christian stronghold in the Maritime Plain on the south towards Egypt.

A.D. 1154.—The famous geographer Idrîsi, who wrote of the Holy City as it was during the occupation of the Crusaders, states that Ghazzah is to-day very populous, and is in the hands of the Greeks (Crusaders). The port of Ghazzah is called Tîda or Taïdâ.

c. A.D. 1160.—Dirghâm, the Egyptian, conquered the Franks in a battle at, or near, Gaza.

A.D. 1170.—After the death of the great Imad ed din Zanki, ruler of Mosul, he was succeeded by his two sons. One of them, Saif ed din Gazi, secured Mosul, and the eastern part of his father's dominions. The other, Nur-ed-din Mohammed, became the chief Moslem prince in Syria, with Aleppo for his capital. In the beginning of December 1170, Nur-ed-din being in the north, Salah-ed-din made a dash against Gaza, and destroyed its suburbs. He plundered the town, but was unable to reduce the fortress.

A.D. 1177.—Salah-ed-din, towards the end of 1177, arrived before Ascalon. The Knights Templars were for the most part in Gaza. The Crusaders came upon Saladin's main body while it was crossing a stream, and was obstructed in its movements by the baggage. The Muslims were easily routed.

A.D. 1187.—After the Battle of Hattin, A.D. 1187, and the surrender of Ascalon to Saladin, Gaza also passed into his hands. It appears also to have opened its gate to Richard I of England for a short time, but it soon reverted to the Muslims.

A.D. 1192.—King Richard, during the third Crusade, took the fortress Dârôn (Latin Darum), built by King Amalrich, a coast city, immediately south of Gaza, after a short siege, and destroyed it.[1]

King Richard reconquered Gaza, placing it in the charge of the Knights Templars, who previously had charge of it.

The walls were dismantled after Richard Cœur de Lion's peace with Saladin, in 1193.

A.D. 1239.—A new Crusade arrived in September 1239. Theobald, Count of Champagne and King of Navarre, was its most important leader. Several hundred knights surprised the Muslims in the neighbourhood of Gaza. The result was a serious disaster. The Latins were attacked and practically cut to pieces on November 13. This rebuff occurred in spite of the remonstrances of Theobald. No precautions having been taken by the Duke of Burgundy, the Counts of Bar and Mountfort, they suddenly found themselves nearly surrounded by the enemy in a narrow pass. There was yet time for them to escape by retreating rapidly by the way in which they had entered; but the majority refused to do this, as inconsistent with the high courage which they professed, and after a desperate struggle Count de Bar was slain, and Amory de Mountfort, with many nobles and knights, were taken captives. The main body of the Crusaders arrived too late to be of any assistance.

A.D. 1242.—Damascus had been in Nejm ed din Ayub's hands during the early part of 1239, and had been taken

[1] See Robinson's *Biblical Researches in Palestine*, vol. ii. p. 38, 1856.

from him by Imad ed din Ismail. In May 1242, the Knights Templars and their Muslim allies defeated an Egyptian army on the borders of Palestine. The Egyptians lost heavily, and were driven back to Gaza, which was their base of operations.

A.D. 1244.—Ayub in his trouble found allies in an unexpected quarter. The Kharezmian Turks had recently been driven from their homes by the Tartar invasion, and were ready to put their swords at the disposal of the highest bidder. These savages, at the invitation of Ayub, entering from the north, flowed like a tide past Safed and Jerusalem, and on St. Luke's Day (October 18, 1244), annihilated the Christian and Saracen armies united for a common cause in the valley of Gaza. History records few more terrible struggles than this decisive battle, which lasted without ceasing from the rising to the setting of the sun, and was renewed on the morrow with the same ferocity. Thirty thousand of the military Orders are said to have been slain; thirty-three Templars, twenty-six Hospitallers, and three Teutonic Knights alone escaped of these brave Orders. The Master of the Temple was amongst the slain, and the Master of the Hospital was amongst those taken captive.

From this blow the Latin Kingdom of the East never recovered. And since this date Gaza has remained a town of comparatively little importance.

A.D. 1250.—King Louis IX (St. Louis of France) and the Mameluke Emirs agreed that all prisoners taken since the Battle of Gaza, in 1244, should be released.

A.D. 1250.—Malek-el-Nâsir of Damascus, as descendant of Saladin, besieged Gaza. Ebek, the first of the Mameluke Slave Dynasty, sent his General Aktai to relieve the city, in which he succeeded.

A D. 1260.—The whole of Palestine was raided by the Tartar invaders, and they stationed garrisons in towns as remote as Gaza.

The Mongols under Hûlagû, sent an Embassy from Gaza, to El-Mudhaffer Kutuy, Sultan of Egypt, demanding his submission.

The Sultan Edh-Dhahir Beibars drove the Mongols out of Gaza.

A.D. 1280.—Kilâwûn, Sultan of Egypt, marched against the Mongols, and encamped at Gaza for fifty days.

A.D. 1291.—The Egyptian Sultan, Melik-el-Ashraf, made Gaza a separate government, and set up a Governor there.

This put an end to the Frank rule in Palestine.[1]

CHAPTER XIV

THE PASHAS OF GAZA

AL NADWAN, and other Pashas, ruled Gaza and all Palestine for more than two hundred years. Under the Sultans of Turkey, these Pashas, seven in number, occupied the city after the crusading period. They began to rule from about A.D. 1510.

They possessed much property in many parts of the country. The present British Consular Agent's house belonged to one of these Pashas.

The old court (serai) belonged to them, and the present barracks.

[1] I am indebted for some of the facts and dates in this chapter to Stevenson's *The Crusaders in the East* (Cambridge: at the University Press, 1907), and Dr. Meyer's *History of the City of Gaza*, Chap. IX.

All the existing fine buildings were erected by them.

The minaret at the Great Mosque, and two other minarets at the Sajaiah, were also constructed in their day.

They governed all Palestine and Syria, having their headquarters in Gaza. Consequently, in the middle of the seventeenth century Gaza once assumed somewhat of its former importance.

Their rule was arbitrary. Pilgrims proceeding to Jerusalem from Jaffa were compelled to get permission from the Pasha at Gaza.

If anyone built a house, or owned anything particularly interesting, the Pashas would lay claim to it by using the expression "Mabrook" (Blessed). If the owner did not reply favourably he was immediately hanged.

Hussein Pasha (*c.* A.D. 1660) made Gaza the capital of Palestine. His serai, which was furnished with great luxury, stood in the middle of a beautiful Gaza garden.[1] One family was called the Frangi. They were the Pashas' gardeners. Their descendants became Muslims.

When the Turks came to Gaza the Pashas only lost the serai and barracks, their other property was not interfered with. It now belongs to their descendants, who are all poor people, and live on their rents.

These Pashas had their own burying ground, which is still seen, and known as the Pashas' cemetery.

Wten Napoleon Bonaparte came to Gaza (A.D. February 1799) the city was not ruled by any power, and the taxes were collected for him by a private individual.[2]

[1] For further information of the beneficent rule of Hussein Pasha, see Meyer, pp. 97, 98.

[2] See Meyer on Napoleon in Gaza, pp. 101, 102.

After the rule of the Pashas, the Muftis governed Gaza—the Turkish Government coming into office in 1852.

It has been extremely difficult to obtain this scanty information about the Gaza Pashas.

CHAPTER XV

DAGON, THE NATIONAL GOD OF THE PHILISTINES

DAGON was represented with the face and hands of a man and the tail of a fish (1 Samuel v. 4). Various kinds of fish were objects of general worship among the Egyptians.

The worship of Dagon did not exclude that of other Baals (2 Kings i. 2, 3). He was eminently the god of agriculture (1 Samuel vi. 4, 5).

The most famous temples of Dagon were at Gaza (Judges xvi. 21, 30) and Ashdod (1 Samuel v. 5, 6). This latter temple was of pre-Maccabean construction, and was destroyed by Jonathan, the brother of Judas the Maccabee (c. 148 B.C.) during the Maccabean wars (1 Maccabees x. 84).[1]

In connection with the history of Samson at Gaza, Mr. R. A. Stewart-Macalister, 1905, explains the architectural character of the Gaza Temple of Dagon. It must have consisted essentially of three members: the cella itself; a very deep distyle portico, and a forecourt,

[1] Josephus, *Antiquities of the Jews*, Chap. XIII. pp. 4, 5. For a complete list of idolatrous observances mentioned in the Old Testament the reader is referred to *The Cambridge Companion to the Bible*, pp. 421–5, 1905.

open to the sky. What seems to have happened was this: the blind prisoner was conducted to the forecourt, whence he could be seen by the Philistine grandees, who sat in the shade of the portico (cf. verse 30, "the house fell *upon* the Lords"), as well as by the large crowd of commoners assembled on the roof. By tricks of strength and buffoonery he was compelled to give them amusement, after which he was allowed to rest awhile, probably in order that he might have strength to continue the sport. He was set to rest between the pillars, which was the nearest place where he could be shaded from the sun's heat while resting. Taking the opportunity, he put forth his full strength, and before the lords of the Philistines realised what he was doing, he was able slightly to displace the posts holding up the portico, but sufficiently to cause them to fall under the weight of the roof.[1]

Colonel Conder remarks it is often denied that the name Dagon applies to the Babylonian and Phœnician deity represented as a merman, with the head and body of a bearded man, and the tail of a fish; because in Semitic speech *Dagon* signifies "Corn." It is, however, recognised that Dagon is the same god, called *Da-gan* in the Akkadian Chronicle of the first dynasty of Babylon; and in Akkadian *Da* signifies "the upper part of a man," while *gan* may be compared with Turkish *kan* for a large fish. Dagon would thus be the same as Oannes (u-khana, "lord of the fish"), a form of the sea-god Ea, who was a man with fish tail. He is represented not only on Assyrian bas-reliefs, but on a seal found near Ashdod in 1875. When the statue of Dagon was broken only the

[1] Twelfth Quarterly Report on the Excavation of Gezer, p. 196. P. E. F.

"fishy part" (dagon) was left. In the Laws of Ammurabi, Dagon is invoked as the deity of regions near the Euphrates, apparently as a water-god.[1]

Prof. Sayce and others now insist that Dagon was not a *fish*-god. The name and worship of Dagon were imported into Philistia from Babylonia.

CHAPTER XVI

THE GAZA JUPITER

THE great statue from Gaza was discovered on September 6, 1879, by the natives at Tell 'Ajjûl, about four miles and a half south of Gaza. Captain Conder, in 1882, reported that we owe its preservation to the exertions of the Rev. A. W. Schapira, the C.M.S. missionary at Gaza. The Arabs had at once commenced to break up the statue, and had suceeded in greatly damaging the face. Mr. Schapira persuaded the Turkish Governor to set a guard over the spot. The antiquarians of Palestine owe him a debt of gratitude for having prevented the entire destruction of this unique monument.

Dr. Meyer, in his *History of the City of Gaza*, Note, on page 153, states that this statue was rescued by the missionary Schapira, and adds in a note on page 156, "that Schapira's connection with the finding of the statue tended at first to discredit the authenticity of the find, because of his previous share in the famous Moabite forgeries. But nothing has ever been advanced to show that this statue shares the character of his other discoveries."

Dr. Meyer is mistaken in attributing the Moabite

[1] *Quarterly Statement* P. E F., Oct. 1909, p. 274.

forgeries to the Rev. Alexander Wilhelm Schapira, who was formerly a Church Missionary Society clergyman at Gaza. It was Mr. M. W. Schapira whose name became connected with the celebrated Schapira collection of forgeries in 1873.

The following appeared in the *Pall Mall Gazette*, November 11, 1879—

"An interesting archæological discovery is reported from Palestine. An Arab who was quarrying stone the other day at a place about four miles and a half from Gaza unearthed a marble figure supposed to be a colossal god of the Philistines. The dimensions of the figure are as follows: Three feet from the top of its head to the end of its beard, twenty-seven inches from ear to ear, thirteen and a half inches from top of forehead to mouth, fifty-four inches from shoulder to shoulder, eighty-one inches from crown of head to waist, and fifty-four inches the circumference of the neck. The total height of the figure is fifteen feet. The hair hangs in long ringlets down upon the shoulders, and the beard is long, indicating a man of venerable age. The right arm is broken in half, while the left arm is crossed over the breast to the right shoulder, where the hand is hidden by the drapery of a cloth covering the shoulders. There is no inscription on the figure, or the pedestal, which is a huge block carved in one piece with the figure. The statue was found in a recumbent position, buried in the sand, on the top of a hill near the sea. It had evidently been removed from its original site, which is unknown. Its estimated weight is 12,000 lbs. The Pasha of Jerusalem has ordered a guard to watch this relic of ancient art, and to prevent any injury to it by the fanatics of Gaza."

Captain Conder, in his notes from Constantinople, July 1882, sent a copy of the sketch which he had made from the original of the Gaza Jupiter in the porch of the Stamboul Museum, which is reproduced in the *Quarterly Statement* P. E. F., July 1882, p. 148.

Conder supposed that the terrible mutilations of this Jupiter may have been effected before the statue was discovered, and it is possible that the pious pagans may have buried their Jupiter to save him from the Christians, and have been obliged to divide it for facility of transport.

CHAPTER XVII

AN OLD SARCOPHAGUS AT GAZA [1]

THE Jerusalem paper, *El-Kuds*, in its issue of February 25, 1910, gave an interesting account of a discovery made at Gaza, and Prof. R. A. S. Macalister has kindly forwarded a translation of the revelant portions of the description. After some remarks on the history of Gaza, the paper proceeds as follows—

"We have been induced to record the above by our having heard that Musa el-Burtu and his partner, Ibn Halaweh, of the people of Gaza, bought land at Gaza for six hundred dollars; and that when Musa went to his land, and was working and digging in it, he found a little door. He entered by it into a cave divided into two chambers, and, entering through the second door, he found a coffin of hard wood. And he opened it, and in

[1] *Quarterly Statement* P. E. F., Oct. 1910, pp. 294-6.

the coffin was another of crystal. And he broke this, and inside it he found one of the old queens embalmed, and on her head a crown adorned with precious stones, and on her neck a necklace of pearls, and three chains besides on her breast; and above her head was a candlestick of gold with a spout, a metre and a half long, and another at her foot a metre long. And he collected all these things and brought them to Beirût, and thence to Egypt; and we have learnt that he sent to his partner in Gaza to pay to the workmen a sum of five hundred napoleons.

"And when the Government heard of this they sent, on their part, a number of people to the said place to preserve and protect it, because the tomb in which the queen was found is of marble, and her portrait is carved on it. And there are other graves besides."

We are, fortunately, able to supplement this by an account sent to us by Mr. Emil G. Knesevich, of Gaza, who has also kindly forwarded a photograph of the sarcophagus.

"At the commencement of 1910, some men were digging out stones in their orange garden, about two miles to the north-west of Gaza, and after reaching a depth of six metres, came upon the ruins of an old door, which led to a big cave about five metres by six metres, and about three metres in height. In the floor and walls of this cave, some tombs were found containing bones, the remains of dead bodies, and a number of idols resembling men, monkeys, eagles, and dogs. These were made of clay and plaster of Paris, and were tinged with a beautiful green tint. In the cave another door was observed; this led to another small cave about two metres by three metres, and two metres in height, in which was found the sarcophagus, of which the following is a description—

"The sarcophagus was by itself in the inner cave, strongly fortified by a sort of a vault built over it of huge stones and plaster of Paris, to prevent it from being damaged. When the stones were removed there appeared this beautiful and remarkable sarcophagus. It was made of pure white marble, and was composed of two pieces, the lid and the coffin. When the lid was taken away, there was found the mummy of a female in a fine state of preservation. The coffin was two hundred and twenty centimetres long, seventy centimetres wide, and seventy-two centimetres high. Unfortunately, the men who found the mummy destroyed it in searching the coffin, hoping to find precious antiques, but they assert that they found nothing, save an artificial tooth attached to a golden wire. Some people say, however, that a book and some precious things were discovered. No inscription of any kind was upon the sarcophagus.

"The lid was beautifully and artistically carved in the exact form of the mummy. Nothing except the head, neck, and shoes were seen, and the rest of the body was carved so as to appear swathed in bandages of linen. The head was neatly fashioned, and the eyes and lips were painted their natural colour. The head was bound with a fillet, the hair was loose and thrown on both sides of the chest. The head, fillet, and the nose suggest that the mummy was a Roman, but the shoes, as carved on the lid, are Egyptian.

"The lower part of the coffin also was cut in the shape of the body, as shown in the photograph. The place that supported the head was carved to resemble the head and neck, and the lower part of the coffin, that rested on the ground, is carved in the shape of the back part of the body. The local government got possession of the

THE MUSLIM MOSQUE—ONCE THE CRUSADERS' CHURCH

[*To face p.* 79

sarcophagus, and dispatched it to Constantinople, together with the remains of the mummy, and the above-mentioned idols, on the 26th of May last." [1]

CHAPTER XVIII

THE GREAT MOSQUE

THE one object of archæological interest in Gaza is the Great Mosque (Djamia el Kebîr) which rises on the top of the hill in the middle of the upper city. This mosque is built upon the site of the Basilica, which the Empress Eudoxia founded, where the Marneion formerly stood, and was built of ancient materials.

In the twelfth century it was a splendid cathedral dedicated to St. John Baptist.

The style of architecture is severe, and the ornamentation very plain. The fine groined roof is entire.

The mosque has three aisles, two of which formed part of the mediæval church.

[1] "A curious seal was, during 1874, found in the vicinity of Gaza. It was in possession of Dr. De Hass, a former American Consul, who gave Lieut. Conder an impression. It represents a human figure with four wings, seemingly like those of a fly or bee, and with a large misshapen human head. In each hand the figure holds an animal resembling an ape, head downwards, being held by the hind leg. Dr. De Hass supposed this to be an effigy of Baal-zebub, god of Ekron, to whom apes were sometimes offered. The seal is square, about one inch wide, and the figure in low relief, roughly cut. A similar seal was found some years ago, and is now in England. It represents a fly or mosquito, with an inscription, the equivalent of the Arabic 'Allah,' perhaps the symbolical effigy of the deity of Ekron."—*Quarterly Statement* P. E. F., Jan. 1875, p. 10.

Rows of pillars, with Corinthian capitals, divide them one from the other.

The roof of the central nave is supported by rows of pillars, one above the other, each pillar of the lower row having a cluster of small marble pillars round it, for greater strength.

One of the upper pillars on the north-east side of the mosque, of grey veined marble, bears a bas-relief of a seven-branched candlestick, with a Greek and Hebrew inscription of three lines inside a wreath. It belongs, as M. Clermont Ganneau surmises, to one of the thirty columns sent by the Empress Eudoxia, and probably comes from the Synagogue of Cæsarea.[1]

The walls and ceiling are now whitewashed. The church was undoubtedly decorated with mosaic and pictures.

The three apses have disappeared to make room for a large octagonal minaret.

On the south side the Moslems have built an additional aisle.

The total length of the building is one hundred and eight and a half feet, interior measure, the nave being twenty-one and a half feet wide, and the aisles thirteen feet.

The west doorway is a beautiful mediæval specimen of the Italian Gothic of the twelfth century churches in Palestine, with delicate clustered shafts and pillars, deeply undercut lily-leaves adorning the capitals.

Lieut. Kitchener, in 1874, took a photograph of the western door as well as the interior of the mosque.

The large marble cruciform font has been removed and

[1] The reader is referred for additional information to Chap. XIV, "Inscriptions," in Meyer's *History of the City of Gaza.*

it now lies in the courtyard adjoining the mosque, where two other Christian symbols may be seen, viz. a bishop's staff, and chalice in marble.

Another view of the history of this mosque is given by the Archimandrite Meletius Metaxakis, in an article on the Madaba Mosaic Map, in *Nea Sion*, March and April 1907, pp. 262–304, in which he states that the modern authors of *Guides to Palestine* hold that the Eudoxian Church is the modern Great Mosque, Djamia-el-Kebîr, taking into consideration, it seems, the information that the Eudoxian Church was to be built in the middle of the city. If, however, we are to accept that the sketch on the chart shows the Eudoxian Church, then we ought to treat the Eudoxian Church as identical, not with the mosque, but rather with the Modern Orthodox Church, built in 1856, during the Patriarchate of Kyrillus II (1845–1872), and through the expenditure of the Brotherhood of the Holy Sepulchre. With regard to its position, the Greek Church is wholly identical with the sketch on the chart.

With regard to the mosque, this is really a three-branched church, being perhaps one of the churches built by Marcian; the columns of this church (having no connection with those from Constantinople for the Eudoxian Church) appear to have been transported from some Hebrew synagogue, perhaps that of Cæsarea, because there is engraved on one of them a seven-branched lamp, under which appears the Hebrew and Greek inscription, "Hananias the son of Jacob."

CHAPTER XIX

GAZA—THE KEY OF SYRIA

GAZA—the outpost of Africa, and the door of Asia—is situated in the south-west of Palestine, and is only about twelve miles to the north of Reifah (formerly Raphia), which marks the Turko-Egyptian boundary, running down to Akaba. Who founded the city is unknown! It is the commercial and administrative centre of all the surrounding sixty-two villages, and for many of the Beduin tribes who pitch their tents in the plains. The area of Gaza is about 2,100 square kilometres. The present city is about two miles from the sea,[1] and lies on an artificial mound which is about 100 feet high above the plain, and 180 feet above the sea-shore. Five minarets break the outline of the flat roofs. There are no scavengers.

The encroachment of the rolling dunes of sand is one of the most serious evils now to be dreaded on the coast of Palestine. Nothing is done to arrest this enemy around Gaza.

The trade and commerce of Gaza are almost exclusively confined to the gathering in and exportation of barley, which is grown on the plain of Philistia, and in the neighbourhood of Beersheba. The majority of the inhabitants of the city and district obtain their livelihood from this trade alone. The widespread olive-grove to the north and north-east, however, creates a considerable manufacture of soap, which Gaza exports in large quantities.

[1] Gaza, like Athens, was purposely built *inland*, for fear of pirates.

The soil is very fertile, but its productiveness is entirely dependent on the rainfall, and in consequence the yield of the crops greatly affects the general condition of the people. The most primitive methods of cultivation are still in general use.

The climate is sub-tropical, and upon the whole healthy. Eye diseases, however, are very prevalent. Malaria and other tropical diseases are also common.

The chief exports besides barley are wheat, millet, and colocynth, while a coasting trade is carried on in "tibn" (chopped straw) and a coarse black pottery, which is the principal manufacture of Gaza, where there is a good market for it. The poor people of the district buy it, and exchange it for cereals and other articles.

From at least 727 B.C. Gaza has been famous for its potteries, of which there are now forty-two within the city. The same method of producing this pottery is used to-day as depicted upon the Egyptian monuments. This manufacture was called "Gazaitæ."[1]

The only other manufactures are a common kind of soap, and cloth, consisting principally of the coarse woollen coats ('abaï) worn by the men. There are also mills for the expression of sesame oil, and for grinding corn.

Cotton goods, and most of the articles necessary for wear, or luxury, are imported. The chief imports from Great Britain are unbleached calicos, which are used by the fellahin for clothing. They are dyed blue locally. Aniline dyes are imported from Germany. The average yearly value of the yarn imported into Gaza and Mejdel

[1] There are seven allusions to potters and potteries in the Old Testament, three in the New Testament, and four in the Deutero-Canonical Books. An excellent photograph of the potter at his wheel is contained in Forder's *Daily Life in Palestine*, Ch. VII. Marshall Bros., Ltd., 1912.

from Manchester is £10,000. The imports are mostly brought from Beirût or Jaffa by small coasting craft, or overland by camels.

The average orange crop of late years has been good. The fruit is excellent. It is better than that of Jaffa, both in taste and in size. Eight thousand boxes were exported, chiefly to Great Britain, in 1910 (valued at £8,000). These orange gardens are gradually increasing, their present number being about twenty. The soil is rich, and excellent for the purpose.

Gaza has no harbour, or any convenient facility for shipping cargo. A pier was constructed in 1906, but it proved a complete failure, on account of its being inadequate to meet the need. It should have been built 120 yards longer. In 1909 the violence of the waves during that winter destroyed about one-third of it.

There is a good deal of surf in the summer, and steamers are often delayed fourteen to twenty days before obtaining their cargo. No regular steamers touch this roadstead, and it is only in summer that these vessels (mostly British) visit it. There is no lighthouse.

It is at this point that the ancient maritime suburb of Mayoumas stood, the concrete remains of which are still visible on the shore.

The population is about 70,000, including the surrounding villages. The fellahin form the bulk of the population—mostly of the poorer classes. The non-increase of population is due to the bad harvests of the last few years. In consequence of the drought in 1905, 15,000 of the city and district, chiefly of the poorer classes, migrated to Jaffa, Haifa, Acre, Nazareth, Damascus and Egypt, owing to the exactions of the Government, and the high rate of interest demanded by the Effendis to whom they were indebted. This exodus is only a temporary misfortune.

The population of Gaza is said at one time to have outnumbered that of Jerusalem.

The road-tracks between Gaza, Jaffa, and Beersheba are badly in need of repair. In places the sand is very heavy, especially in the summer-time. A road tax is levied, but no road has been improved for many years.

Gaza is in a state of lethargy for about nine months out of twelve, until the middle of April, when the barley crop is cut, because most of the inhabitants earn their living by the barley trade. In consequence of much idleness during this slack period, drunkenness is not an uncommon vice. The wealthy merchants buy at harvest-time large quantities of barley, which are generally exported or stored, until the prices in Great Britain and Egypt are high, when they sell to British and other purchasers. The poorer traders pitch small tents in the neighbourhood of the city, and among the Beduins, to whom they sell clothes, sweets, coffee, and other articles, taking barley in exchange. When they have secured a sufficient amount, they sell it either to the agents of the European merchants, or to the native merchants of the city. Any one who visits Gaza in June and July will be astonished to see the large quantities of barley heaped upon the sea-shore, awaiting the arrival of steamers.

The building of the Government hospital, talked of for so many years, has been begun, but it has, so far, made little progress.

No banks are permanently established in Gaza. All money transactions are carried on through the banks of Jaffa.

There is a growing desire for male education. The

citizens, in September 1911, enthusiastically encouraged a public performance of *Hamlet*, on behalf of a native Muslim school. It was a first and successful attempt of the kind.

Many Jews have been making inquiries with the view of purchasing land in this district, and especially over the boundary at Reifah.

Meyer says that during the Hellenistic period the Jews resorted to the Gaza fairs. Frequent mention is made of these fairs by Rabbinical authorities. In fact the fairs at Gaza were always famed throughout Palestine.

Until the last seven years the numerous hordes of 100,000 Beduins within the Beersheba district were under the government of Gaza. They swarm the desert towards the south in the winter months, and then move northwards, up the Philistia plain, for herbage.

Even in Christian families, until about thirty years ago, slaves were sold in Gaza.

The cattle of Gaza are few, and there is scarcely any export. Camels are common. They number approximately 6,700, including those of the surrounding villages and Beduins. Sheep and goats number approximately 171,000, together with those of the near villages and Beduins. Oxen number approximately 10,000 in and around the city. They are chiefly used for ploughing. Horses and mules and donkeys are not numerous, but the former have an excellent reputation throughout Palestine. Carriages usually belong to Jaffa, and carry back in eleven hours passengers from Gaza. The first motor-car, owned by a German from Jaffa, reached Gaza during April 1912, accomplishing the journey in three hours, and returning the same day.

Jackals and foxes are numerous. Quails arrive from Egypt in July and August.

CHAPTER XX

GARDENS—OLIVE-GROVES—BIRDS, ETC.

In January 1884, Mr. H. Chichester Hart visited Gaza, and contributed a valuable paper to the *Quarterly Statement* of the Palestine Exploration Fund, October 1885, entitled "A Naturalist's Journey to Sinai, Petra, and Southern Palestine." From Chapter XI, Gaza to Jaffa, I cull a few items of general interest—

"Gardens of fruit-trees, olive-groves, and enclosures, hedged by the prickly pear, reached our camp from the inland side. The trees at Gaza are chiefly date-palms,[1] olives, sycamore-fig, carob or locust-tree, and fig; a very handsome tamarisk reaches a height of thirty or forty feet, and has light green foliage, very refreshing and home-like after the dull grey or lifeless green of the desert. The olives are of enormous age. They usually have unbranched trunks, two or three feet in height, then perhaps divided, and at seven or eight feet the leafy canopy, browsed below to a level height by cattle, begins. The average height of the tree is twenty to twenty-five or thirty feet. Old trees have often mere shells of their trunks remaining. I measured the two largest I saw, a few miles north of Gaza; their girth was eighteen and twenty feet respectively at two feet from the ground, a size which was maintained, or very nearly so, till the trunk forked."

Gaza is quite embowered in these great olive-groves,

[1] The palm is the tree of the desert. It grows luxuriantly not only in the rich soil of Egypt, but in the sandy borders at Gaza.

which stretch north-eastwards the whole four miles to Beit Hanûn.

These magnificent groves are the largest in Palestine. They are said to have been planted by the Greeks, and it is asserted that at all events since the coming of the Saracens some seven hundred years back, not a single new tree has been planted. Most of the trees stand on huge roots, and have evidently sprung up from the remains of former trunks rotted away.

Lentils are a common crop. Gaza trades with an excellent quality of barley to Egypt. Consequently, wealth increases, but the population, being still in a low state of civilisation, live poorly. Even the well-to-do have as a daily meal "fûl" (beans) with an onion, and a piece of roughly ground barley bread. Meat is not wanted.

The luxuriance of the gardens and orchards, remarkable for the scarlet blossoms of the pomegranates, and the enormous oranges which gild the green foliage of their groves, is due to the abundance of water, drawn from twenty wells of fresh water bursting from the sandy soil—some of them are not less that 150 feet deep. The natives greatly prize the quality of the water. Good water is, indeed, plentiful at greater or less depth over all the district, even on the sea-shore, though the frequency of rubble cisterns to the south and east show that in ancient times the inhabitants depended largely on artificial supply.

Gaza and Ascalon have always been noted for their wells.[1]

[1] It is remarkable that both the two celebrated early Palestinian wells noted in the old Testament are still in existence: (1) Abraham's well at Beersheba (Gen. xxi. 30); and (2) the well of Bethlehem, for whose water David thirsted (1 Chron. xi. 17).

In and about the Gaza olive-groves, several birds familiar in Great Britain abound. There are English sparows, swallows, buntings, goldfinches, black redstarts, chaffinches, stonechats, willow-wrens, chiff-chaffs, blackbirds, and hooded crows. Other birds seen are Egyptian kites, buzzards (common species), "boomey" or little southern owl, red-breasted Cairo swallows, pelicans, dunlins, calandra and crested larks, bulbuls, pied-chats, and Menetrie's wheatear.

Frequently dogs with unmistakable traces of jackal parentage are seen. It is by no means uncommon for these vagrant animals to interbreed along this part of the Mediterranean seaboard.

At the risk of some repetitions, I have gladly availed myself of the opportunity of making use of a few details published in the late Annual Reports by Mr. A. A. Knesevich, H.B.M. Consular Agent at Gaza.

During my first visit to Gaza, in July 1891, my tent was pitched in the Muslim cemetery, which stretches over a wide space on the west of the city. The graves are generally covered by a small erection of mud-brick, plastered over and whitewashed. The cemetery is not enclosed by any fence.

CHAPTER XXI

HISTORY OF THE GAZA MISSION OF THE CHURCH MISSIONARY SOCIETY (1878–1912)

THE Muslim city of Gaza (in Arabic *Chazzeh*) was visited by the late Rev. F. A. Klein during a tour of investigation in 1862.

Later on a pressing invitation was received from the inhabitants to open a school in their midst.

A catechist was sent to make inquiries, but nothing more was then done.

In 1878, however, the C.M.S. took over the four schools, two for boys and two for girls, containing some 250 to 300 children, and other work which had been started and carried on for several years by Mr. Pritchard, a gentleman of independent means, who had settled in Gaza. Shortly afterwards the Rev. A. W. Schapira entered into residence. He opened a reading-room, which attracted even higher-class Muslims.

Notwithstanding a temporary opposition, the Kaimakam, on Christmas Eve, 1880, addressed the gathering, and encouraged the school.

Medical work was started about 1882, and was the first C.M.S. work of the kind in Palestine.

The dispensary received a gift from the late Rev. John Venn, of Hereford, and a fund was raised in Salisbury Square for establishing a permanent medical mission.

In 1886 the late Rev. Dr. R. Elliot took charge.

Dr. H. J. Bailey was also temporarily at this post in 1890, in order to assist in the medical work.

During this period Dr. Elliot had the joy of baptising, on October 12, 1890, Moorjan and Mehbruki, two of his own servants, man and wife, natives of the Sudan.

Some years before they had been sold in Gaza as slaves, the man for ten pounds, and the woman for twice that sum. The slave market has been abolished for about twenty years.

All this time the medical work was confined to the treatment of out-patients, but in March 1891 a hospital adapted from a native house was opened.

Medical itineration now began to be undertaken at Mejdel and Ashdod. The fame of the hospital spread far and wide.

The Rev. Dr. Sterling (the author of *A Grammar of the Arabic Language*, and *Arabic and English Idiom—Conversational and Literary*) arrived in 1893, and his predecessor, the Rev. J. Huber, of German nationality, who built the ladies' house and church room, entered into rest on July 18, and his body was buried in the cemetery in the mission compound.

Other branches of the work have prospered. In 1902 the numbers in the girls' school rose from sixty-eight to three hundred, and have now increased to four hundred. The Sunday school has increased proportionately with the day school. It would be difficult to find more interesting schools in Palestine, so efficiently superintended by Miss Smithies, who is ably assisted by her own trained staff of native teachers.

In 1906 the Muslims presented Dr. Sterling, on behalf of the building fund of the hospital, with £100, which they had subscribed in token of their gratitude for his work among them.

The leavening influence of Christian teaching is unquestionably having far-reaching effects.

Dr. Percy W. Brigstocke was appointed, in 1907, to act as colleague with Dr. Sterling, but he was transferred to Es Salt at the end of 1911.

The old hospital and out-patient hall were insanitary, and much too small for the work, therefore it was with thankfulness that the Bishop in Jerusalem dedicated the new hospital, containing forty-six beds, on April 1, 1908.

The opening of the spacious out-patient block took place on February 22, 1911.

The patients are drawn from all classes, Muslims, Orthodox Syrians and Jews. They may be seen sitting side by side in the out-patient hall waiting for the doctor, who is an accomplished Arabic scholar.

During 1912 there were 29,581 attendances of out-patients, 701 in-patients, 452 visits in town, and 411 major operations.

The fees from the in-patients and out-patients during 1912 amounted to £326 18*s*. 10*d*., which goes to assist in the upkeep of the hospital.

There is an out-station, for the expenses of which Dr. Sterling is responsible, at El Arish, the ancient Rhinocolura, "the River of Egypt" (Numbers xxxiv. 5; Isaiah xxvii. 12), a town of twelve hours' ride from Gaza, where the C. M. S. school has had an average attendance of fifty pupils. The population is entirely Muslim.

Mr. W. Watson, of Newcastle-on-Tyne, has done heroic service not only by inspiring others to give and help the completion of the hospital and out-buildings, but also in attending personally to the purchasing of much building and furnishing material.

How much Gaza owes to him and his Northumbrian

helpers will only appear when the great audit of all things takes place.[1]

Canon Sterling is largely his own clerk of the works. He is to be congratulated that after twenty years of missionary and medical work in Southern Palestine, he has been enabled to complete the group of medical and educational buildings which now adorn the C. M. S. Gaza compound.

CHAPTER XXII

EL ARÎSH AND C.M.S. MISSION

The border town of Egypt, El Arîsh, seventy miles south of Gaza, is generally identified as the "River of Egypt," which was the most southern boundary of the Holy Land in patriarchal times. At present the actual boundary between Palestine and Egypt is a line running from Rafah, the ancient Rhaphia, some thirty miles to the north of El Arîsh, to Akaba.[2]

The country between Rafah and El Arîsh is desolate. The large sand dunes, the dust of ages, have encroached

[1] Adapted from *Handbooks of the C. M. S. Missions, The Palestine Mission*, 1910, a typewritten document by Dr. Sterling, 1912, and *Mercy and Truth*, 1911.

It may not be generally known that General Gordon paid two visits to Gaza in 1883. On the first occasion he spent a fortnight, and afterwards three weeks in the C. M. S. compound. An interesting relic is the iron bedstead on which he slept. It is still associated with his name, and is being carefully preserved.

[2] For additional information see Palmer's *The Desert of the Exodus*, vol. ii. pp. 286–8.

upon the land, whereas the Land of Promise may be recognised by its fertility. Around the villages which lie between Gaza and Rafah are orchards which produce an abundance of fruit; the fig, vine, pomegranate, almond, olive, apricot, date, mulberry, palm, apple, orange, and banana, are all grown, besides vegetables of all kinds, of a size rarely met with in Great Britain.

El Arîsh, the ancient Rhinocolûra, the chief town of the Sinai Peninsula, possesses some eight thousand inhabitants. The "River of Egypt," so called, is conspicuous by its absence, except in the rainy season, when a large portion of the water from the peninsula courses through its bed to the sea. The river-bed is very wide, and many hundreds of poplar trees are scattered over it, with numerous wells for irrigation.

The most striking building is the Government Fort. It is some five hundred years old, and bears evidence of attacks made by invaders.

Owing to the barrenness of the land the people are exempted from all taxation. Some five thousand camels are owned by these Sawârikeh Beduins, and these "ships of the desert" do much of the carrying trade between Egypt and Syria, and in Egypt itself during the cotton season.

The people are exclusively Muslims, with the exception of two Coptic officials. The town is beautifully clean.

There is here a magnificent field for missionary enterprise. No mission work of any kind had ever been attempted in the town until Dr. Sterling opened a boys' school in 1906.

The people are friendly, and come to the hospital at Gaza in goodly numbers.

In 1908 Dr. Sterling was able to purchase a beautiful site of four and a half acres. A native master from

Gaza, M. Nasri, and pupil teacher, are now at work in a school attended by sixty or seventy scholars. This school is dependent upon voluntary help, and Mr. W. Watson and Dr. Sterling are responsible for its maintenance.

Not only is Holy Scripture taught, but the master has many opportunities of bearing witness to the truths of Christianity.

This station ought to be properly supported, and can be more easily worked from Gaza than from Egypt.

Dr. Sterling has the plans for building schools for boys and girls, a teachers' house, a house for dispensary attached for two English ladies, preferably one an educationalist and the other a nurse. At present there is only money in hand for the proposed girls' school.

I am indebted to three numbers of *Jottings and Snapshots from Gaza, Southern Palestine*, for some of the above information.

NOTE.—On Feb. 20, 1799, Napoleon Bonaparte took El Arîsh. At the capitulation of the town the French were permitted to evacuate Egypt with all the honours of war.

APPENDIX I

PUBLIC GAMES AT GAZA [1]

PERIODICAL games were often closely connected with the religious rites. The great importance of public games in Imperial times is well known. Not a provincial town of any consequence was without them. This was especially the case with those in connection with the games in honour of the Emperor, which were everywhere in vogue, even in the time of Augustus.

In Gaza a *πανήγυρις* Ἁδριανή (an assembly of a whole nation for a public festival) was celebrated from the time of Hadrian. A *παγκράτιον* (the joint contest which comprises both wrestling and boxing) is mentioned as held there in the inscription of Aphrodisias. These wrestlers and boxers of Gaza were, in the fourth century, the most famous in Syria. St. Jerome, in his *Life of St. Hilarion*, mentions the Circensian games there.[2]

Pharisaic Judaism has always repudiated this heathen kind of games (1 Maccabees i. 14, 15; 2 Maccabees iv. 9–17).

Judaism, however, was unable, in spite of this theoretic repudiation, to prevent the pageantry of heathen games from developing every fourth year, in

[1] For this information I am indebted to Schürer's *History of the Jewish People in the Time of Christ.*

[2] See "Circus, games of," *A Dictionary of Classical Antiquities*, etc. London: Swan Sonnenschein & Co., Ltd., 1891.

the midst of the Holy Land, during and after the Herodian period.[1]

THE CIRCUS OF GAZA [2]

Moonrise on the desert. Above the dark ridges of rocks which rose from the tawny waste of sand, a pale faint light poured down on the wilderness of Gaza. An aged man, yet apparently more worn with labour than with years, was standing at the entrance of a cave, which, dark and silent, pierced one of the mountain ridges.

The time of which I am speaking was about 350 years after the birth of our LORD; the place was one of the deserts which stretched themselves between the Nile and the Holy Land. Already innumerable hosts of monks occupied the wilderness of Egypt; and if St. Antony had attained the greatest reputation for the holiness of his life and the wonders of his miracles, St. Hilarion among the monks of the solitudes held the second place. Many times he had fled from the concourse of people that the fame of his powers of healing had drawn to him; and now, in one of the wildest and most unfrequented parts of the wilderness, he hoped to find a place where he might serve GOD without the interruption of men.

The moonlight showed distinctly the furthest objects on the horizon; and as the hermit stood gazing around him, and thinking, perhaps, of that new heaven and new earth wherein dwelleth righteousness, which shall be the

[1] For a description and plans of Herod the Great's *Theatre* (not Amphitheatre as in text) outside Jerusalem, see Herr Schick's Report, *Quarterly Statement* P. E. F., July 1887, pp. 161–6.

[2] This tale (No. X) by the late Dr. Neale appears in his *Lent Legends: Stories for Children from Church History.*

abode of those who have been CHRIST's faithful servants here, he noticed a dark spot in the far distance, which gradually drew nearer, and took form and shape.

Half-an-hour brought to the entrance of his cave a large company of Christians. Camels there were to carry those who were of rank to need such a conveyance, and attendants and slaves in abundance. For already, in part, the kingdoms of this world were become the kingdoms of our LORD and of His CHRIST; and to be a Christian was no longer, as fifty years before it had been, a badge of infamy; although in the south-western part of Palestine the worshippers of idols still outnumbered the holders of the true faith.

"Are we happy enough," said one of them who arrived first, a tall and somewhat portly man, who had just descended from his camel before speaking; "are we happy enough to stand in the presence of Hilarion, of whose fame all Egypt and Palestine are full?"

"My name is Hilarion, my son," said the hermit; "and if ye seek anything with so miserable a sinner as myself, I am ready, GOD helping, to assist you so far as may lie in my power, He enabling me."

"Well, then, this is the case," said the stranger. "I am a citizen of Gaza; my name is Italicus; and I come to you for that which may much assist in promoting the glory of Him that is our LORD and SAVIOUR."

"If it be to His glory, my son," said Hilarion, "ask what you will, and in His Name I promise to fulfil, so far as I may, your desires."

"I will tell you, holy father," said Italicus. "It is the custom of our city that the two most wealthy inhabitants should try the speed of their horses against each other in the circus. Now, for this year I am appointed to exhibit these races on the one side, and Ælius Flaccus, who is a worshipper of idols, on the other. He has dedicated his horses and his chariots to the ancient idol of the city, Marnas, and he boasts that no Christian can conquer those which have been so consecrated. All our fellow-citizens know me to be a Christian; they know that I put my only trust in our LORD whom the Gentiles blaspheme; and they know also that the horses of Flaccus are the best breed in the country, and that mine, although I have done my best, are inferior, and give no promise of victory. Wherefore I have betaken myself to you, holy father, to entreat you to assist me, if it may so be, in this great strait."

"And are you not ashamed," said Hilarion, "to trouble a servant of CHRIST with matters such as these? Why not, rather, sell your miserable horses, and give the price of them to the poor? according to that saying, 'Sell that thou hast, and give to the poor, and thou shalt have treasure in heaven.'"

"But, my father," returned Italicus, "you must consider that this office is none of my seeking; it is thrust upon me by the laws of the city. I desire not victory for mine own honour; but the heathen look upon this race as a trial between Marnas and the GOD whom the Christians worship. It is for CHRIST's sake, not for mine, that I desire the victory."

"Is this so?" inquired Hilarion, looking round on the little company that had gathered about him.

"It is so," said an old Christian, stepping forward from the rest. "It is no vainglory that brings us hither; we who have seen the true glory of the martyrs of Palestine, who by divers torments rendered up their most blessed souls to GOD. It is as Italicus says. The horses of

Flaccus are dedicated to Marnas; they are the fleetest that the whole province of Palestine can show; those of Italicus, though he has done his best, cannot be compared to them; and yet the voice of the people has consecrated them to the GOD whom we worship. For any common victory we should not have sought assistance from you; as it is, we do not think that we are preferring an unworthy request. If Flaccus wins, Marnas conquers also; if Italicus is first in the race, then, as the multitude will deem, the LORD CHRIST will show Himself to be superior to the idols of the heathen."

"It is a hard case," said Hilarion, "when such rivalships find place. Nevertheless we must not quench the smoking flax. All that a Christian man may lawfully do to destroy the works of the devil, that it is the bounden duty of Italicus, and of myself, and of every one that bears the name of CHRIST, to take in hand. Wherefore bring me a bowl of water."

One of the attendants ran to the little stream by which the hermit had taken up his abode, filled a vessel, and brought it to him. He made the sign of the cross over it and drank.

"Now, my son," he said to Italicus, "take this water and sprinkle your horses, and their manger, and their stable therewith. Thus you shall find in the day of trial, that the meanest of GOD's servants, even though he be like myself, has power to confound the idol Marnas, and all his priests, and all his worshippers."

Thankfully and carefully Italicus received the water; and after expressing his gratitude to the hermit, he and his company returned over the desert towards Gaza.

Now we will pass over ten days.

A bright spring morning shone over the ancient city of

the Philistines. Here and there the white marble temples of Jupiter, and of Minerva, and of Apollo, glittered in all the beauty of their pillars, and their friezes, and their bas-reliefs. But high above the rest, and more sumptuous than all, glowed that of the god Marnas, the idol whom the inhabitants of Gaza delighted to honour. Had you stood by the great door of his temple, you might have seen a crowd of worshippers and a little company of priests offering their sacrifices, and praying that he would be pleased to prosper his own worshippers on his own day; that he would give fleetness to their horses; and that he would assist in rooting out the execrable sect of the Nazarenes and their crucified GOD from the face of the earth. The oxen were garlanded with flowers, the altars were wreathed with laurel, and the augurs were taking omens as to the success of the contest. The laurel leaves when cast into the fire gave a good omen; the chickens when fed at their troughs promised victory; and from the large size of the heart in one of the sacrificed beasts, the soothsayers drew the conclusion that the god had bid Ælius Flaccus to be of good courage.

The report had spread through the city that Hilarion the wonder-worker had interested himself in the success of the Christian. Half-an-hour before midday crowds were flocking to the circus; the pagans, who were of the Red faction, wearing badges of that colour, and outnumbering their opponents, who were of the Green party, six or seven to one. They flocked in through the various doors of the circus; the officers whose duty it was marshalled the way for the more influential citizens; the poor locarii, who had come early to take the best places, sold them at the best bargain they could to the wealthier spectators; and so great was the interest in a contest, not so much between Italicus and Flaccus as between Marnas and the GOD of the Christians, that never had so brisk a trade been driven in the letting and underletting of seats as on that day.

I have many times described to you the amphitheatres as they were in that age. Now I will tell you what the circus was like; and attend, or you will not understand the story.

Imagine a long oval space of ground, a quarter of a mile in length, and surrounded with seats, rising in tiers, one above the other, the lowest of stone and the highest of wood; these tiers of seats were divided by narrow passages called *vomitories*, which gave entrance to the spectators. At one end of the enclosed space was a wooden erection, containing a series of wooden seats, or rather boxes, handsomely curtained and cushioned, for the use of the magistrates. As it is not yet the hour of the race we shall be able, as we enter, to examine the place without disturbance. This spot, immediately in front of the magistrates' seats, is the starting-place for the chariots; they call it the *carceres;* in front of it, you see, are four images of Mercury, with chains stretched from one to the other, behind which the horses will presently be stationed; the men standing by them, two of the Red, two of the Green faction, are called the *moratores;* their business is to see that it is a fair start. From the carceres, as you will observe, there runs almost to the other end of the circus a very broad brick wall, some three feet high, and twelve in thickness; at both ends of this are three little pyramids, which they call *metæ;* the wall itself they name the *spina.* The horses, then, starting from the carcer, under the magistrates, run seven times round the spina, going in what seems to us a very unnatural fashion, from left to right. In order that there may be no mistake, that man who is leaning idly against the spina, and chatting with one of moratores, has it in charge to set up a little wooden obelisk close to the carcer—you will see the sockets in the ground—for each turn that the chariots make. Thus, when the Red horses have made one circle, he will erect a red obelisk; when the Green ones have done the same, a green one, and so on.

Now all the seats are so full that it seems impossible for more spectators to be accommodated; nevertheless, still they come pouring in. It is not only from Gaza and the neighbouring country that they are flocking, but from Joppa, from Cæsarea, and even from Ælia Capitolina—as they now call Jerusalem—many of its inhabitants are come up to these games. The priests of Marnas will feast for many a day on the proceeds of this; and if it should so happen that the horses of Marnas conquer, his worshippers will say, what King Darius said to another idol, "Great art thou, O Bel, and there is no deceit in thee!" As to Didymus the Christian priest, he had at first held back from expressing any interest in the matter; but when he was told that Hilarion had consented to assist Italicus, he encouraged to the best of his powers the Christian candidate, and though he would not himself attend the games, he awaited the result in his own house with no small anxiety.

Now the magistrates are taking their places in their robes of office. He in the centre, who has just taken his seat in that projecting balcony, is Asinius Gallus, edile of the place; a noted favourer of the old religion, and the great friend of Flaccus. Next to him are the principal magistrates of some of the neighbouring towns; and on each side of them, the inferior officials of Gaza itself. There also are Italicus and Ælius Flaccus; but of the twenty or thirty persons who thus occupy the seats of honour, not more than three are of the Green faction.

Presently, the doors under the balcony occupied by the magistrates, and opening on the hither end of the circus, are thrown open; and the chariots and horses enter. The moratores cast lots for the respective position of each. For, as you will see, the chariot that was on the left, or, as we should now call it, the near side, had the disadvantage of being compelled to make a larger circle each time; this was, however, a little made up for by the danger that the chariot on the off side experienced in rounding the metæ at the end. They cast two pieces of ivory into a bowl, and shook them; that which bore the name of Flaccus first leaped out; his morator had therefore the choice of ground; and his chariot took the right-hand place.

These chariots, as you see, have only two wheels, are low, have the front part bulging out in a circle, and are entirely open behind; they are intended only to carry one man. As that of Ælius Flaccus takes up its position, the Red faction through the circus rise, clap their hands, stamp with their feet, and cheer. And well they may; for every one agrees that finer animals than the three black horses yoked abreast which draw it were never seen in Gaza. There is also some applause bestowed on the three bay horses of Italicus, but poor and faint indeed, as compared with the thunder that had greeted the other. As you may well imagine, their master has carefully observed the directions of Hilarion; horses and manger and provender have been sprinkled with the water; and Italicus himself entertains not the least doubt of success; though the edile of Joppa has just offered to him of Lydda an even bet that the red chariot will have finished its seventh course before the green has reached the mèta which will form its sixth and a half. Now, silence; for Asinius Gallus is about to speak. His voice can only be heard down a short space of that enormous length; but the purport of what he says is soon passed on to its very extremity.

"Good men and true,"—such are his words—"it is well known to all that this city of Gaza has been for now many hundred years a worshipper of the great god Marnas, and that we, the larger part of its citizens, still cleave to the religion of our forefathers. It is also well known to all that, as elsewhere throughout the world, so here more especially, there are not wanting those who ridicule our faith, they themselves worshipping One that was crucified in this land, more than three hundred years ago. These games, therefore, which we are this day met to celebrate, have more than the common interest that in other years we have taken in them. Our worthy fellow-citizen, Ælius Flaccus, has dedicated his horses to Marnas, and the soothsayers have assured him of victory. His rival, who follows the faith of the emperors, Junius Italicus, has in like manner sought the assistance of his God, and has availed himself of I know not what incantations performed by one of the savage and brutish race of men now beginning to people the wilderness to the south. Thus this day will be made manifest which of these two gods can best hear the prayers of his servant. As a magistrate of this city, I am bound to judge and decide impartially; but as a believer in our ancient faith, I am not ashamed to express my hope that Marnas will vindicate his honour by giving the victory to his worshipper. And this, men of Gaza, I know to be your wish as well as my own; the soothsayers have given us the promise of success; our god himself is on our side; and the prayers of all that have the ancient fame of Gaza at heart will be joined with mine that Ælius Flaccus may prove the victor in this race."

The people, of course, applauded loudly; and Asinius Gallus resumed his seat. Immediately, the moratores disengaged the chains from the images of Mercury; the drivers grasped their reins and their whips; deep silence fell upon the multitude; and the edile again stood up, and gave the white napkin, which was the signal for the start, to the official whose business it was to make the sign. He then, mounting on the spina, stood a little before the two chariots, holding the linen in his hand, and keeping his eyes fixed on Asinius Gallus. The magistrate, after having cast his eyes right and left to see that his brother functionaries were comfortably settled, and ready to look on at their ease, nodded to the officer; the napkin fell; and the chariots started.

Inferior as were the horses of Italicus to those of his opponent, the spectators had imagined that for the first three or four courses round the circus the race would be closely contested. But scarcely had a minute elapsed, when the green chariot, surrounded by whirlwinds of dust, was already half-way to the further meta, while that which had been dedicated to Marnas, in spite of the vociferations and lashings of the driver, was lagging far behind. Those at the further end of the circus fancied that its driver, secure in the excellence of his horses, had given his rival a long start, in order to make his own victory the more triumphant. But those who could see better were not so deceived. Flaccus and the edile interchanged glances of astonishment and vexation; one or two of the other magistrates whispered to each other that it must be witchcraft; it was in vain that the Reds shouted, clapped their hands, and endeavoured to encourage the charioteer; vast majority as they were, their voices were drowned in the thunder of applause which welcomed the green chariot as it now flew towards the carceres, having made one circle, while the other had scarcely yet turned the meta at the further end. Up went the green obelisk; and the Christian chariot started on its second course. It was in vain that Ælius Flaccus stamped with rage, ground his teeth, and shook his fist at his own unfortunate driver, now creeping up towards the magistrates' seat. As of old time, the chariot drave heavily; and even from some of the Red faction there burst forth a shout of "Marnas is conquered!" But when the green chariot, now making its fifth round, passed its rival which had not yet completed its fourth, such a thunder of applause echoed through the circus as Gaza had never heard before—unless it might be when, some fifteen hundred years further back, Samson had made sport for the lords of the Philistines on the roof of the temple of Marnas, then better known by his other name of Dagon. The priests of the idol will do well to treasure up the offerings they have received to-day; for, depend upon it, they will never have any more. I can already hear some words that sound exceedingly like "Impostor!" in the mouths of their adherents; and now that the green chariot comes bounding along to the conclusion of its final course, and its driver throws his reins into the hands of the morator, and leaps, well pleased, to the ground, and it is evident to all that the horses are not distressed, and have scarcely even turned a hair, while those of Marnas are labouring at the further end of the circus, and have its full length to traverse before they finish their sixth course—now I say, that the idol has been utterly confounded, and the faith of one poor hermit has triumphed over all the charms of a college of pagan priests, the shout that bursts from every part of the benches seems to me to ring the death knell of idolatry in Palestine.[1]

[1] The Editorial Secretary of the *Society for Promoting Christian Knowledge* informs me that "No permission is required to reprint from Neale's *Lent Legends*, as the copyright has now expired." It was written at Sackville College in 1855, and reprinted in 1905 by the S.P.C.K.

APPENDIX II

DESTRUCTION OF THE EIGHT HEATHEN TEMPLES OF GAZA (A.D. 401)

DURING the Episcopate of St. Porphyrius, A.D. 395–420, there were eight State-property temples in the city of Gaza: (1) Helios—the Sun; (2) Aphroditus—Venus; (3) Apollo; (4) Persephone; (5) Hecate; (6) the Hiereion (or Heroon); (7) the Tychæon; (8) the Marneion.

Their names imply that purely Greek worship prevailed in them.

1. THE TEMPLE OF THE SUN.—In Greek mythology the sun-god, son of the Titan Hyperion and the Titaness Theia, is himself often called Hyperion.

Helios was worshipped in many places. The Island of Rhodes was entirely consecrated to him. The worship of this sun-god was with great difficulty eventually suppressed by substituting for him the prophet Ἡλίας. In modern times Helios seems to be identified with St. Elias, whose chapels are built chiefly on hill-tops.

It was this particular worship to which the Antonines showed special favour. The name of Antoninus Pius is connected with the building of the Temple of the Sun at Baalbec.

The late Lieut. Conder wrote an interesting article on "Sun Worship in Syria," in the *Quarterly Statement* of the P. E. F., April 1881, pp. 80–4. Prof. Sayce, in

Patriarchal Palestine, p. 218, ed. 1912, states that with both the Semites of Babylonia and of Canaan the supreme object of worship was Baal or Bel, "the Lord," who was but the Sun-god under a variety of names.[1]

2. APHRODITE (called *Venus* by the Romans).

In Greek, the goddess of love and beauty.

The worship of the Phœnician goddess Astarte, brought in by Phœnician traders in early days, helped to form the conception which the Greeks had of Aphrodite.

A Sanctuary of Aphrodite (Astarte) stood on the place where, according to Christian tradition, was the Sepulchre of CHRIST.

A chief worship of Ascalon was that of 'Αφροδίτη Οὐρανία, *i.e.* of Astarte, as Queen of Heaven. Herodotus mentions her as the deity of Ascalon.

This female deity is represented on coins of the Imperial epoch chiefly as the tutelary goddess of the City.

As goddess of the *sea*, and maritime traffic, especially of calm seas, and prosperous voyages, she was widely worshipped by sailors and fishermen as the goddess of *calm*.

Her influence was also felt in the gardens among the flowers in the spring-time. It was then that her principal festivals occurred.

A chief seat of her worship was Cyprus.

Additional information on this independent, unmarried goddess is to be found in Sayce's *Patriarchal Palestine*, pp. 218–21.

3. APOLLO (Greek 'Απόλλων), son of Zeus and Leto, brother of Artemis, portrayed with flowing hair, as ever being young.

Apollo appears originally as a god of *light*. As the god

[1] A few traces of the cult of Baal and Astarte are to be found in England.—*Quarterly Statement* of P. E. F., Oct. 1909, pp. 280–4.

of spiritual light, his festivals are all in spring and summer. He is one of the great gods of the Greeks, and next to Zeus the most widely worshipped.

Josephus speaks of a Temple of Apollo at Gaza, 96 B.C. (*Antiq.*, xiii. 13, 3), at the time when the city fell into the hands of Alexander Jannæus. "The Senators, who were in all five hundred, fled to Apollo's Temple (for this attack happened to be made as they were sitting), whom Alexander slew."

The worship of Apollo is to be traced to Seleucid influence, for Apollo was the ancestral god of the Selucids, and a great favourite with them.

3. PERSEPHONE (Latin Proserpina), daughter of Zeus and the earth-goddess Demeter, the goddess of the lower world.[1]

Her special name in Attic cult is CORÊ, lit. "the maiden."

Persephone is emblematic of vegetable life that comes and goes with the changing seasons.

Her festivals were celebrated in spring, and after the harvest.

The pomegranate was Proserpine's symbol, and the pigeon and the cock were sacred to her.

5. HECATE, a Greek moon-goddess, perhaps of non-Hellenic origin. Her appearance is frightful. She is generally represented as a daughter of Perses.

As a goddess of the lower world she was the patroness of all enchanters and enchantresses, who were her disciples and protegés.

6. HEROON. THE HIEREION.

Heroon is the shrine of a hero, from ἥρως, a hero.

[1] See the story of Demeter and Persephone in Neale's *Stories of Heathen Mythology*, pp. 102–10. S.P.C.K. 1905.

Hesiod reserves this name for mortals of divine origin, who are therefore also known as demigods.

7. THE TYCHE, identified with the Roman Fortuna. A female deity—the daughter of Zeus. She was of more importance in Italy than among the Greeks.

In Greek mythology she was originally the goddess of chance. In the course of time she came to be extensively worshipped as a goddess of prosperity, who had cities under her special protection.

Meyer (pp. 122 and 158), refers to the Tyche as a familiar figure upon Gazæan coins, having a woman's head, with a turreted crown consisting of three towers, one of which is pierced with a door, and with a veil over the back of her head.

The reverse side of the coin of Antoninus in Plate XI, No. 7, of De Saulcy's *Numismatique de la Palestine*, is a good representation of the Gaza Tyche.

8. THE MARNEION.

The Temple of Marnas is spoken of as the Marneion, a home of the city's god.

Marnas was the Baal of Gaza.

In the Roman period Marnas was the chief deity of the city. St. Jerome mentions this Temple of Marnas.

The oldest express testimony of the cult of Marnas is, according to De Saulcy, that of certain coins of Hadrian, with the superscription GAZA MARNA.

"In the last days of paganism, as we learn from Marcus Diaconus, in his *Life of Porphyry of Gaza*, this great god of Gaza was regarded as the god of rains, and invoked against famine. That Marnas was lineally descended from Dagon is probable in every way, and it is therefore interesting to note that he gave oracles, that he had a circular temple, where he was sometimes worshipped by human sacrifices, that there were twenty wells in the sacred circuit, and that there was also a place of adoration to him, situated, in old Semitic fashion, outside the town." [1]

This temple outside the town was possibly the place called Bethelia, one and three-quarter miles north of Gaza.

[1] *Encyclopædia Britannica*, vol. xviii, ninth edition, p. 756.

APPENDIX III

PASSAGES OF THE HOLY BIBLE, THE DEUTERO-CANONICAL BOOKS, AND THE NEW TESTAMENT

INDEX

INDEX

Milton Keynes UK
Ingram Content Group UK Ltd.
UKHW022002221123
433079UK00006B/453

9 781022 123274